Implementing and Sustaining Your Strategic Plan

Implementing and Sustaining Your Strategic Plan

A Workbook for Public and Nonprofit Organizations

**John M. Bryson,
Sharon Roe Anderson, and
Farnum K. Alston**

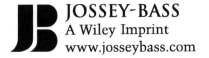
JOSSEY-BASS
A Wiley Imprint
www.josseybass.com

Contents

PART 4   RESOURCING AND STRUCTURING IMPLEMENTATION, ALIGNMENT, AND ONGOING LEARNING   147

Preface

Strategic planning is "a deliberative, disciplined effort to produce fundamental deci-sions and actions that shape and guide what an organization (or other entity) is, what it does, and why it does it" (Bryson, 2011). Strategic planning is now standard practice for a substantial majority of public and nonprofit organizations. But only those organizations that successfully implement their plans fulfill their missions, meet their mandates, and create significant and lasting public value. *Implementa-tion*, in other words, is "the effort to realize in practice an organization's mission, goals and strategies, the meeting of its mandates, continued organizational learn-ing, and the ongoing creation of public value" (Bryson, 2010). Implementation is thus more time consuming and resource intensive than strategic planning. Indeed, most organizations spend most of their time implementing their strategies, not coming up with new ones, and that is as it should be. That ongoing work of mak-ing things happen and satisfying key stakeholders is the *busy-ness* from which business—whether corporate, government, or nonprofit—gets its name.

But strategic planning and implementation do overlap—and necessarily so—in significant ways. For example, strategic planning should be informed by what has worked and not worked for the organization in the past, and plans should always be developed with implementation in mind. *Implementing and Sustaining Your Strategic Plan* is designed to help practitioners ensure that the hopes and dreams embodied in strategic plans are realized in the nitty-gritty world of implementa-tion. The workbook is thus a companion not only to *Strategic Planning for Public and Nonprofit Organizations*, fourth edition (Bryson, 2011), which over the course of its four editions has helped to make strategic planning a conventional feature of management practice, but also to *Creating Your Strategic Plan* (Bryson & Alston, 2011), a companion workbook focused on plan creation, now in its third edition. A new workbook is needed both because implementation is a big enough task that it deserves its own workbook and because the implementers of strategic plans are often not the same people as the strategic planners.

The basic approach to implementation outlined in *Strategic Planning for Public and Nonprofit Organizations* has proven as useful today as when the book was first published. However, the field has changed as the world of theory and practice has evolved. The latest edition of that book and both workbooks embody much of what has been learned by scholars and practitioners and by the authors' own practice.

Why has strategic planning become standard practice for most public and nonprofit organizations? There are a variety of reasons. First, many public organizations are now required by law to conduct strategic planning, and many nonprofit organizations are required to do so by their funders. Second, strategic planning is now seen as a mark of good professional practice, so organizations pursue it to enhance their legitimacy and standing in the eyes of external audiences. And many organizations simply copy what everyone else is doing. But we believe the most important reason strategic planning is so widely used is that public and nonprofit leaders find that it can help them think, act, and learn strategically—precisely what is required as these leaders grasp the challenges their organizations face, figure out what to do about them, and follow through with effective implementation.

Strategic planning is thus a crucial component of *strategic management*, defined as "the integration of strategic planning and implementation across an organization (or other entity) in an ongoing way to enhance the fulfillment of mission, meeting of mandates, and sustained creation of public value" (Bryson, 2010). Taking a strategic management approach that links strategic planning with effective implementation is a must if these organizations are to compete, survive, and prosper; meet their legal, ethical, professional, organizational, community, and public service obligations successfully; and create significant and lasting public value and advance the common good. The basic logic of strategic management is presented in Figure 1. It involves creating public value, meeting mandates, and fulfilling one's mission via effective implementation of new and ongoing strategies—and exiting as gracefully as possible from the doing of low-priority or ineffective things. Figuring out which strategies to keep, which to add, and which to drop is the job of strategic planning.

Implementing and Sustaining Your Strategic Plan is meant to serve several purposes.

- It is designed to help public and nonprofit organizations (or collaborations or communities) as they build and deploy needed capacities to successfully implement their strategic plans and align themselves to produce continuous learning and long-lasting public value.

- It provides a conceptual framework, vocabulary, step-by-step approach, adaptable worksheets, and supplemental resource materials that allow users to custom design their implementation strategies to meet their unique needs over the life of their strategic plan.

FIGURE 1

The Basic Logic of Strategic Management

Creating lasting and
significant public value

Meet mandates ← → Fulfill mission

Achieve goals

Implement ongoing and new
strategies, stop doing low-priority
things, and manage the organization
in an ongoing strategic way

Manage portfolios of new
initiatives, including new or → Sustain and improve
revised programs and projects → ongoing strategies ← Quit doing lowest
and operations priority things

Formulate and adopt strategies
likely to be effective; identify what
is low priority or just doesn't work
and figure out how to quit doing it

- It is meant to be a resource throughout the time frame of the organization's strategic plan—these days that is usually three to five years at most. During this time, plan and strategy refinement and reassessment will typically occur on a regular basis, and it is not unusual for new strategic plans to be developed before the three- to five-year period is up.

This workbook's conceptual framework, step-by-step process, and worksheets can be used in a variety of ways. For example:

- The workbook as a whole or selected parts of it can be used by elected or appointed policy boards, boards of directors, senior management teams, implementation teams, and task forces on a regular basis throughout the process of sustained implementation (for example, it could be part of regularly scheduled meetings).

- The workbook's parts can also be used with strategy-specific workgroups at various points in an implementation process.

- Individual worksheets or combinations of worksheets can be used to address a variety of implementation-related tasks on an as-needed basis. These tasks include

  Clarifying desired implementation outcomes and the time frames and action steps necessary to achieve them

  Attending to the full array of guidance, control, and performance management approaches necessary to ensure that needed implementation successes and ongoing learning occur (Simons, 1995)

  Building ownership with stakeholders so they know and own the plan and can engage in continuous implementation via achievement of short-term milestones

  Making goal achievement a part of the organization's daily way of working and a prominent feature of its culture, rather than seeing implementation as just dealing with annoying add-on projects

  Building in the forums needed to foster a habit of dialogue and inquiry and the real learning that results from such forums

  Relying on appropriate decision-making methods, including collective decision making when appropriate

  Organizing and providing necessary resources to teams as major implementation vehicles

  Fostering leadership, professional, and ongoing organizational development as a part of the implementation process

  Attending to functions and operations that may not be highlighted in the strategic plan

  Identifying, building, and maintaining needed core organizational competencies

  Clarifying where formative and summative evaluation processes of key implementation elements should occur and what their main focus should be

  Preparing for the next round of strategic planning

- Finally, the workbook can be used as part of for-credit courses and noncredit professional development programs focused on strategic planning, strategic management, or implementation.

This workbook addresses key issues in the design of an overall implementation process. Although it touches on some of the same issues that are important in strategic planning, it does so only where implementation and strategic planning issues clearly overlap. We therefore recommend that this workbook be used in tandem with the fourth edition of *Strategic Planning for Public and Nonprofit Organizations* (Bryson, 2011); the information in that book will place the workbook's guidance and worksheets in a broader context, provide information on other significant issues, review relevant details, and alert users to important caveats. We also recommend that organizations use this workbook in tandem with the third edition of the workbook *Creating Your Strategic Plan* (Bryson & Alston, 2011), so that planning and implementation can be more seamlessly pursued. Furthermore, we emphasize that this workbook is not a substitute for the internal or external professional consultation and facilitation services that are often needed during a strategy implementation effort. The implementation process is both important enough and difficult enough that having support from someone who has "been there and done that"—and who thinks wisely and reflectively about the process—may make the difference between a successful, high-value effort and one that stalls or fails or, even though completed, does not produce much of value.

Audience

This workbook is intended mostly for leaders, board members, elected officials, managers, planners, employees, and other stakeholders of public and nonprofit organizations and communities. Businesses may also find the workbook useful if their organizations have a direct business relationship with public or nonprofit organizations or if they find the approach generally applicable to their organizations. The audience for this workbook therefore includes

> People interested in understanding more about strategy implementation for their public and nonprofit organizations, collaborations, or communities
>
> Sponsors, champions, and funders of strategy implementation processes
>
> Portfolio, program, and project managers charged with overseeing important aspects of implementing strategic plans
>
> Implementation teams and task forces
>
> Implementation consultants and process facilitators
>
> Teachers and students of strategic management

Where This Workbook Will Be Relevant

This workbook is designed to be of use to a variety of people and groups:

> Public and nonprofit organizations as whole entities (rather than their parts)

Parts of public and nonprofit organizations (departments, divisions, offices, bureaus, units)

Programs, projects, business processes, and functions (such as personnel, finance, purchasing, information management) that cross departmental lines within an organization

Collaborations involving programs, projects, business processes, and services that involve more than one organization and possibly more than one sector

Networks or groups of organizations focused on cross-cutting functions or issues

Communities

The worksheets generally assume that the focus of the implementation effort is an organization. Please tailor and modify them appropriately if your focus is different.

How This Workbook Facilitates Strategic Plan Implementation

This workbook makes implementation easier in several ways, including the following:

The implementation process is *demystified* and made understandable and accessible. Although we have taken the risk of simplifying a complex process, this approach draws on best practices from many organizations and important findings from implementation research.

Fears about the process are allayed through the presentation of a simple, flexible model; step-by-step guidance; and easily understood worksheets.

Implementation process sponsors, champions, coordinating committees, consultants, and facilitators are provided with many of the tools they will need to guide an organization or group through a strategy implementation process.

The complex process of strategy implementation has been broken down into manageable steps, making the overall process easier to manage.

Use of the workbook can document progress and keep the process on track.

Communication among process participants is made easier by the workbook's structured approach. Tangible products emerge from completing the worksheets, including the products necessary to develop a variety of implementation plans. These products can guide the dialogue and decision making necessary for successful implementation.

Overview of the Contents

This workbook is divided into five parts, each devoted to a major *function* (or *action category*) necessary to produce desirable outcomes. We argue that if these functions are fulfilled (or the action categories are effectively pursued), then the organization will implement its strategies and strategic plan; meet its mandates, fulfill its mission, and achieve its goals; and as a result, significant and lasting public value will be created (see Figure 2). Each function encompasses from one to five steps in an overall twelve-step process that we call the Implementation Cycle, which is discussed in detail in Step 1. The steps may be thought of as significant design features of an implementation process. The entire process must be responsive to the context within which it takes place. The five functions are

- Understanding implementation and assessing readiness

  Step 1: Understanding implementation and assessing readiness

- Getting organized

  Step 2: Leading implementation

  Step 3: Understanding how and why the strategic plan came to be

  Step 4: Clarifying who the implementation stakeholders are

- Clarifying strategic and operational directions

  Step 5: Articulating what the organization's mandates, mission, vision, and values mean for implementation and alignment

  Step 6: Getting clear about strategies that will continue, will be started, and or will be phased out

- Resourcing and structuring implementation, alignment, and ongoing learning

  Step 7: Budgeting the work

  Step 8: Creating an implementation management structure

  Step 9: Developing effective implementation teams

  Step 10: Organizing alignment and learning processes

  Step 11: Putting it all together in strategy maps and action plans

- Maintaining, readjusting, or terminating strategies

  Step 12: Staying the course—or changing it

The workbook ends with supportive resources, a glossary, and a bibliography.

FIGURE 2

The Implementation Cycle and Chapter Outline

Purpose or Desired Outcomes: Creating Public Value — Meeting Mandates, Fulfilling Mission, and Achieving Goals — Implementing the Organization's Strategies and Strategic Plan

Major functions (or categories of actions) required to produce desired outcomes	Understanding Implementation and Assessing Readiness	Getting Organized	Clarifying Strategic and Operational Directions	Resourcing and Structuring Implementation, Alignment, and Ongoing Learning	Strategy Maintenance, Readjustment, or Termination
Process design features	**Step 1:** Understanding implementation and readiness assessment	**Step 2:** Leading implementation **Step 3:** Understanding how and why the strategic plan came to be **Step 4:** Clarifying who the implementation stakeholders are	**Step 5:** Articulating what the organization's mandates, mission, vision, and values mean for implementation and alignment **Step 6:** Getting clear about strategies that will continue, will be started, or will be phased out	**Step 7:** Budgeting the work **Step 8:** Creating an implementation management structure **Step 9:** Developing effective implementation teams **Step 10:** Organizing alignment and learning processes **Step 11:** Putting it all together in strategy maps and action plans	**Step 12:** Staying the cource—or changing it
Process context					

Acknowledgments

JOHN WOULD LIKE TO THANK the people with whom he has worked over the years on various strategic planning and implementation projects. He has learned a great deal from them and appreciates their willingness to help him understand more about strategic planning and implementation and how to make them more effective. He would also like to thank all the people who have taken his classes and workshops in strategic planning. And he is especially appreciative of Sharon Roe Anderson's and Farnum Alston's contributions and willingness to bring their insights, experience, and talents to bear on this workbook project. Sharon has been a close colleague, friend, and partner in producing many programs, projects, and publications over the years, of which John is quite proud. She is a perfect gem. Farnum is also a valued friend and the coauthor of the companion workbook *Creating Your Strategic Plan*, third edition (2011). He is also quite obviously a master strategic planning practitioner and theorist who has field-tested key parts of this workbook in an extraordinary number of settings. Finally, John would like to heartily thank Barbara Crosby for her special insights, constant encouragement, and love throughout the process of developing this workbook; and he offers many thanks to the other members of his delightfully expanding family, which now includes a grandchild. They provide more than enough inspiration to work for a better future for us all.

SHARON THANKS the outstanding professionals and reflective practitioners she interviewed in preparation for this book: Jennifer Ringgold, Minneapolis Park and Recreation Board; Jocelyn Hale, The Loft Literary Center; Randall Johnson, Twin Cities Metropolitan Council; Susan Neis, Cornerstone; Susan Mundale, Osher Lifelong Learning Institute; Julia Classen, Aurora Consulting; Leah Goldstein Moses, The Improve Group; John Schultz and Yvonne Selcer, Hopkins (Minnesota) Public Schools; Theresa Pesch, Children's Hospitals and Clinics of Minnesota; Denise Mayotte, Sheltering Arms Foundation; and Stephen Troutman, IBM. She also thanks John Bryson and Barbara Crosby for their friendship, good conversations, and encouragement. She offers her thanks, too, to the many community leaders who have invited her to participate in their organizations. Their hard work and commitment to the public good has enriched and enhanced her life. Finally, Sharon thanks her terrific husband, Roger, and son, Colby, for their love and genuine interest in her work.

FARNUM WOULD FIRST LIKE TO THANK his family—his wife, Kirsten, and his daughter, Greer, for their love and support and their giving up of family time to allow him to continue to collaborate with John, and now Sharon, on this new workbook. He would next like to thank the many colleagues, clients, and friends who, over thirty-five years and now over 400 major organizational change management and strategic planning projects, have been the real-life inspiration for his work and his contribution to this workbook. Their hands-on involvement in public, private, and nonprofit organizations and their belief in better governance, quality leadership, integrity, honesty, and the need to add real value have been invaluable to him and to his contribution to this book. The colleagues include (among many) Ansel Adams, Senator Dianne Feinstein, Steve Born, Bud Jordahl, Dale Stanway, William Bechtel, and Dave Schwartz. Special thanks go again to John Bryson. After thirty-seven years of friendship we have come together for a second workbook. John's contributions to and insights about improving public and private organizations, their leadership, and good governance have helped us all.

April 2011

John M. Bryson
Minneapolis, Minnesota

Sharon Roe Anderson
Eagan, Minnesota

Farnum K. Alston
Bozeman, Montana

The Authors

John M. Bryson is McKnight Presidential Professor of Planning and Public Affairs in the Hubert H. Humphrey School of Public Affairs at the University of Minnesota. He works in the areas of leadership, strategic management, and the design of organizational and community change processes. He has consulted with a wide range of government, nonprofit, and business organizations in North America and Europe. He wrote the best-selling and award-winning *Strategic Planning for Public and Nonprofit Organizations*, now in its fourth edition (2011), and cowrote, with Barbara C. Crosby, the award-winning *Leadership for the Common Good*, now in its second edition (2005). He is a Fellow of the National Academy of Public Administration.

Bryson has received many awards for his work, including four best book awards, three best article awards, the General Electric Award for Outstanding Research in Strategic Planning from the Academy of Management, and the Distinguished Research Award and the Charles H. Levine Memorial Award for Excellence in Public Administration given jointly by the National Association of Schools of Public Affairs and Administration and the American Society for Public Administration (ASPA). In 2011 he received the Dwight Waldo Award from ASPA. The award honors persons who have made "outstanding contributions to the professional literature of public administration over an extended scholarly career of at least 25 years." He serves on the editorial boards of the *American Review of Public Administration*, *International Public Management Journal*, *Public Management Review*, *International Review of Public Administration*, and *Journal of Public Affairs Education*.

He earned his undergraduate degree in economics from Cornell University, and he holds MS and PhD degrees in urban and regional planning and an MA degree in public policy and administration, all from the University of Wisconsin.

Sharon Roe Anderson is an expert in collective leadership—people doing together what they could not do as individuals. Her pragmatic approach makes her sought after as a strategist and coach in the areas of leadership, change management, facilitation, and community and organizational development. She has more than thirty-five years of experience in developing programs for people at all levels in the educational, political, governmental, community, and business arenas. She facilitates and consults around issues related to strategic planning, team building, facilitation, nonprofit board governance, and implementation. She is and has been a member of many nonprofit boards of directors. Her background includes extensive public affairs work in executive and professional development, international and intercultural relationships, and leadership education. She is a coauthor of two University of Minnesota Extension Service publications, *Leadership for the Common Good Fieldbook* (2000) and *Facilitation Resources* (1999).

Prior to cofounding the successful firm Aurora Consulting in 2002, Anderson was director of professional development programs at the Humphrey School of Public Affairs at the University of Minnesota. She has also directed the institute's Reflective Leadership Center and its International Fellows Programs.

She obtained her BA degree in mathematics from St. Olaf College and her Master of Liberal Studies degree from the University of Minnesota.

Farnum K. Alston is the founder of The Crescent Company—750 Black Bear Road, Bozeman, Montana 59718; phone: (406) 600-6622; e-mail: f.alston@comcast.net. He established this company in 2000 to assist public, for-profit, and nonprofit organizations and also individuals with change management and strategic planning projects. Alston has, over the last forty years, worked on over 400 major change management and strategic planning projects for public, private, and nonprofit organizations. He has been a managing director for The International Center for Economic Growth and has served on many public and nonprofit boards and committees, including the Government Finance Officers Association (GFOA) award committee, the Baldrige National Awards evaluation committee, the Henry's Fork Foundation board (an environmental protection organization), the Going To The Sun Rally board (a nonprofit that raises money for good causes), and as an appointed member of several school district boards. He is also a recipient of the U.S. Department of Commerce Outstanding Service Award.

Alston has had extensive government experience at the federal, state, regional, and local levels. He served as (in chronological order) environmental adviser to Governor Patrick Lucey of Wisconsin, staff director of the Upper Great Lakes Regional Commission, director of the Federal Upper Great Lakes Regional Commission (appointed by Presidents Ford and Carter), deputy chief administrative officer for the City and County of San Francisco, and deputy mayor and budget director for Dianne Feinstein when she was mayor of San Francisco.

Alston has also had extensive business experience, including being involved with over 200 major governmental and business consulting projects while working with Woodward Clyde Consultants; being a partner at KPMG Peat Marwick, where he led that organization's government and higher education sector practices; and being the founder and owner of The Resources Company and The Crescent Company.

Alston did his undergraduate work at the University of California, Berkeley, in economics and his postgraduate work at Montana State University and then at the University of Wisconsin, Madison, in public policy.

Part 1

Understanding Implementation and Assessing Readiness

1
Understanding Implementation and Assessing Readiness

Step 1A: Understanding what it takes to successfully implement strategies and strategic plans

Step 1B: Assessing readiness for implementation

Understanding Implementation and Assessing Readiness

Purpose of Step

Just creating a strategic plan can produce significant value for an organization—as long as the plan has emerged from a deliberative process involving key stakeholders making use of relevant analyses and syntheses of appropriate information. A good strategic plan will clarify organizational purposes, directions, goals, and ways of achieving them. A good strategic planning process will also build intellectual, human, social, political, and civic capital. *But that is not enough!* Effectively implementing strategies, programs, projects, action plans, budgets, learning practices, and other implementation components will bring the strategies to life and create more tangible value for the organization (or collaboration or community) and its stakeholders as mandates are then met, the mission is fulfilled, and the goals are achieved. An effective implementation process is needed to coordinate and align the mission, mandates, systems, strategies, budgets, programs, projects, operations, and activities of the numerous executives, managers, professionals, technicians, frontline practitioners, and other stakeholders likely to be involved. The implementation process must also allow for ongoing learning and readjustments as new information becomes available and circumstances change—that is, as hopes and dreams encounter realities on the ground. Blending what is intended with what is possible and what emerges along the way will constitute the real meaning of implementation for the organization and its stakeholders. Helmut von Moltke, the Prussian army chief of staff from 1857 to 1888, captured the need for strategic adaptability in combat situations with two now famous aphorisms: "No plan survives contact with the enemy," and "Strategy is a system of expedients" (quoted in Hughes, 1993, pp. 45, 47). Although workbook users are highly unlikely to be in combat situations, the advice to attend to shifting contexts and to be adaptable regarding means—and perhaps ends—is well taken.

Successful implementation helps to complete the move from strategic planning to strategic management. *Strategic planning* may be defined as "a deliberative, disciplined effort to produce fundamental decisions and actions that shape and guide what an organization (or other entity) is, what it does, and why it does it" (Bryson, 2011, p. 26). *Implementation* overlaps with strategic planning, but focuses on the effort to realize in practice an organization's mission, goals, and strategies; the meeting of its mandates; continued organizational learning; and the ongoing creation of public value. *Strategic management* is "the integration of strategic planning and implementation across an organization (or other entity) in an ongoing way to enhance the fulfillment of mission, meeting of mandates, and sustained creation of public value" (Bryson, 2011, p. 26). But effective integration of strategic planning and implementation does not happen by chance—although good fortune can certainly help. Douglas Adams, author of *The Ultimate Hitchhiker's Guide to the Galaxy*, notes how ill-conceived or poorly integrated plans and implementation approaches can lead to bemused disengagement or perhaps resigned defeat, when he says, "I love deadlines. I love the whooshing sound they make as they fly by" (Adams, 2002, p. ix). Effective strategic management does not happen by accident—it must be planned for and pursued in practice in an interactive, learning-focused, and results-oriented way.

A Brief Review of the Strategy Change Cycle

This workbook is a companion to *Strategic Planning for Public and Nonprofit Organizations*, fourth edition (Bryson, 2011) and to another workbook, *Creating Your Strategic Plan*, third edition (Bryson & Alston, 2011). *Strategic Planning for Public and Nonprofit Organizations* provides a detailed overview of and guidance on how to design an effective strategic planning and implementation process and is illustrated with several real-life examples. *Creating Your Strategic Plan* focuses on helping users develop a strategic plan, with less attention paid to implementation. *Implementing and Sustaining Your Strategic Plan* complements that workbook by specifically addressing the challenges of implementation.

The Strategy Change Cycle serves as an organizing framework for the book and both workbooks, so it makes sense to briefly review it now before focusing specifically on implementation. The Strategy Change Cycle has proven its worth for many public and nonprofit organizations as a conceptual and practical guide that helps them meet their mandates, fulfill their missions, and create public value. The ten steps of the cycle are

1. Initiating and agreeing on a strategic planning process

2. Clarifying organizational mandates

3. Identifying and understanding stakeholders and developing and refining mission and values

4. Assessing the environment to identify strengths, weaknesses, opportunities, and challenges (threats)

5. Identifying and framing strategic issues

6. Formulating strategies to manage the issues

7. Reviewing and adopting the strategic plan

8. Establishing an effective organizational vision for the future

9. Developing an effective implementation process

10. Reassessing strategies and the strategic planning process

The Strategy Change Cycle is presented graphically in Figure 3, and the steps are described briefly in Exhibit 1. The steps in the cycle are meant to guide organizational members as they

- Organize effective participation
- Create meritorious ideas for mission, goals, strategies, actions, and other strategic interventions
- Build a winning coalition
- Implement their strategies
- Build capacity for ongoing implementation, learning, and change

FIGURE 3

The Strategy Change Cycle

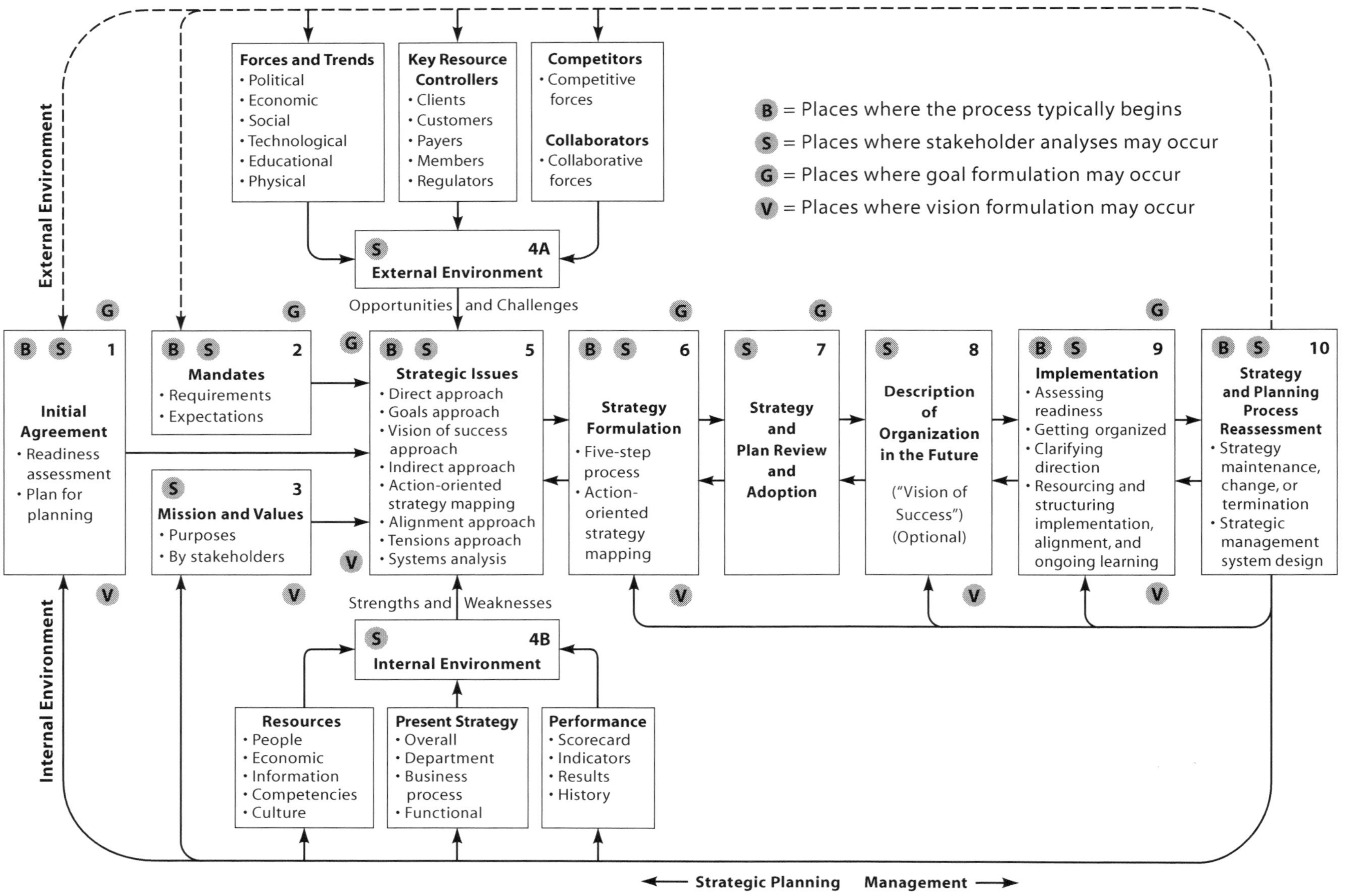

Ⓑ = Places where the process typically begins
Ⓢ = Places where stakeholder analyses may occur
Ⓖ = Places where goal formulation may occur
Ⓥ = Places where vision formulation may occur

External Environment

Forces and Trends
- Political
- Economic
- Social
- Technological
- Educational
- Physical

Key Resource Controllers
- Clients
- Customers
- Payers
- Members
- Regulators

Competitors
- Competitive forces

Collaborators
- Collaborative forces

Ⓢ **4A External Environment**
Opportunities and Challenges

Ⓖ Ⓑ Ⓢ **1 Initial Agreement**
- Readiness assessment
- Plan for planning

Ⓑ Ⓢ Ⓖ **2 Mandates**
- Requirements
- Expectations

Ⓢ Ⓥ **3 Mission and Values**
- Purposes
- By stakeholders

Ⓖ Ⓑ Ⓢ Ⓥ **5 Strategic Issues**
- Direct approach
- Goals approach
- Vision of success approach
- Indirect approach
- Action-oriented strategy mapping
- Alignment approach
- Tensions approach
- Systems analysis

Ⓖ Ⓑ Ⓢ **6 Strategy Formulation**
- Five-step process
- Action-oriented strategy mapping

Ⓢ **7 Strategy and Plan Review and Adoption**

Ⓢ **8 Description of Organization in the Future**
("Vision of Success") (Optional)

Ⓖ Ⓑ Ⓢ **9 Implementation**
- Assessing readiness
- Getting organized
- Clarifying direction
- Resourcing and structuring implementation, alignment, and ongoing learning

Ⓑ Ⓢ **10 Strategy and Planning Process Reassessment**
- Strategy maintenance, change, or termination
- Strategic management system design

Internal Environment

Ⓢ **4B Internal Environment**
Strengths and Weaknesses

Resources
- People
- Economic
- Information
- Competencies
- Culture

Present Strategy
- Overall
- Department
- Business process
- Functional

Performance
- Scorecard
- Indicators
- Results
- History

← Strategic Planning   Management →

External Environment

Internal Environment

EXHIBIT 1

Steps in the Strategy Change Cycle

STEP 1: Initiate and Agree on a Strategic Planning Process

Step 1 involves negotiating an agreement with key internal (and possibly external) decision makers or opinion leaders on the overall strategic planning process, the desired outcomes, the schedule, the key planning tasks, and the likely requirements for success.

The strategic planning process agreement itself should cover

- The purpose of the effort
- A statement (however sketchy) of desired outcomes to be achieved
- Preferred steps in the process
- The schedule
- The form and timing of reports
- The role, functions, and membership of any group or committee authorized to oversee the effort (such as a strategic planning coordinating committee)
- The role, functions, and membership of the strategic planning team
- The likely requirements for success
- Any important limitations or boundaries on the effort
- Commitment of resources necessary to proceed with the effort

STEP 2: Clarify Organizational Mandates

The purpose of this step is to clarify the formal and informal mandates placed on the organization (the *musts* and *must nots* it confronts) and to explore their implications for organizational action.

STEP 3: Identify and Understand Stakeholders, Develop and Refine Mission and Values, and Consider Developing a Vision Sketch

A stakeholder is any person, group, or entity that can place a claim on the organization's attention, resources, or output or that is affected by that output. The key to success for public and nonprofit organizations is the ability to address the needs and desires of crucial stakeholders—according to those stakeholders' criteria.

The organization's mission, in tandem with its mandates, clarifies why it exists and its principal routes to creating public value. Any government, agency, nonprofit organization, or corporation must seek to meet certain identifiable social or political needs. Viewed in this light, an organization must always be considered the means to an end, not an end in and of itself.

The mission statement developed and refined in this step should grow out of a thorough consideration of who the organization's (or community's) stakeholders are. The organization's value system might also be identified, discussed, and documented. The organization may also wish to create a sketch of its *vision of success*, to guide subsequent planning efforts.

STEP 4: Assess the Environment to Identify Strengths, Weaknesses, Opportunities, and Challenges

In this step the strengths and weaknesses of the organization are assessed and their strategic implications noted. This may include identifying the organization's distinctive competencies—that is, those abilities that enable it to perform well in terms of key performance indicators (or critical success factors), especially when compared to its competitors. In addition, the opportunities and challenges (or threats) facing the organization are explored, and again, strategic implications are recognized.

STEP 5: Identify and Frame Strategic Issues

Together, the first four steps of the process lead to the fifth, the identification of strategic issues—the fundamental challenges affecting the organization's mandates, its mission and values, its product or service level and mix, its costs, its financing, its structure, its processes, and its management.

STEP 6: Formulate Strategies to Manage the Issues

Strategies are the means by which an organization intends to accomplish a goal or reach an objective. A strategy summarizes a pattern across policy, programs, projects, decisions, and resource allocations developed to deal with the issues identified in Step 5. Strategies may be of several types:

- Grand (or umbrella) strategy for the organization, collaboration, network, or community as a whole
- Strategy for organizational subunits
- Strategies for programs, services, products, or business processes
- Strategies for functions such as human resource management, information technology, finance, and purchasing

These strategies can be used to set the context for other change efforts aimed at restructuring, reengineering, reframing, repurposing, or otherwise changing the organization.

Steps 1 through 6 may be thought of as strategic *planning*, whereas Steps 7 through 10 are more about *management*. All the steps together may be thought of as a *strategic management process*.

STEP 7: Review and Adopt the Strategic Plan

The purpose of this step is to gain a formal commitment to adopt and proceed with implementation of the plan(s). This step represents the culmination of the work of the previous steps and points toward the implementation step, in which adopted strategies are realized in practice. Formal adoption may not be necessary in all cases to gain the benefits of strategic planning, but quite often it is.

STEP 8: Establish an Effective Organizational Vision for the Future

An organization's vision of success outlines what the organization should look like as it successfully implements its strategies and achieves its full potential. Such a description, to the extent that it is widely known and agreed on in the organization, allows organizational members to know what is expected of them without constant direct managerial oversight. This description also allows other key stakeholders to know what the organization envisions for itself. Visions of success actually may be developed at several places in the process. Most organizations, however, will not be able to develop an effective vision of success until they have gone through strategic planning more than once. Thus their visions of success are more likely to serve as a guide for strategy implementation and less likely to be a guide for strategy formulation.

STEP 9: Develop an Effective Implementation Process

In this step adopted strategies are implemented throughout the relevant systems. An effective implementation process and action plan must be developed if the strategic plan is to be something other than an organizational New Year's resolution. The more that strategies have been formulated with implementation in mind and the more active the involvement of those required to implement the plan, the more successful strategy implementation is likely to be.

STEP 10: Reassess Strategies and the Strategic Planning Process

The purpose of the final step is to review implemented strategies and the strategic planning process. The aim is to find out what worked, what did not work, and why, and to set the stage for the next round of strategic planning.

This workbook attends in detail to *the last two steps* of the Strategy Change Cycle: how to develop an effective implementation process and how to review and reassess strategies in practice and the strategic planning process.

Desired Implementation Outcomes

Lasting and significant *added public value* is the most important implementation outcome that leaders, managers, and planners should seek from reasonably smoothly and rapidly meeting the organization's mandates, fulfilling its mission, achieving its goals, and in general satisfying key stakeholders. Achieving this overarching outcome will come about via these more instrumental outcomes:

- Creation and maintenance of the coalition necessary to support and implement the desired changes. The coalition may already exist; if not, it will have to be created. The size and shape of this coalition will vary depending on the nature of the changes being sought.

- Avoidance of the typical causes of failure (which may be seen as barriers or roadblocks to achieving the overarching outcome). These causes are legion, but include the following:

   Failure to maintain or create the coalition necessary to protect, support, and guide implementation.

   Failure to plan carefully for implementation.

   Resistance based on attitudes and beliefs that are incompatible with desired changes. Sometimes these attitudes and beliefs stem simply from the resisters' not having participated in strategy or plan development.

Personnel problems such as inadequate numbers, poorly designed incentives, inadequate orientation or training, or people's overcommitment to other activities or uncertainty that involvement with implementation can help their careers.

Incentives that fail to induce desired behavior on the part of implementing organizations or units.

Implementing organizations' or units' preexisting commitment of resources to other priorities and a consequent absence of uncommitted resources to facilitate new activities; in other words, there is little "slack" (Cyert & March, 1963).

The absence of administrative support services.

The absence of rules, resources, and settings for identifying and resolving implementation problems.

The emergence of new political, economic, or administrative priorities.

- Development of a clear understanding among implementers of what needs to be done and when, why, and by whom. Statements of goals and objectives, a vision of success, clearly articulated strategies, and educational materials and operational guides all can help. If they have not been created already, they may need to be developed in this step. Subsequent steps in the implementation process and accompanying worksheets will assist you in developing them. These statements and guides will help to concentrate people's attention on making the changes that make a difference as adopted strategies are reconciled with existing and emergent strategies.

- Use of a *debugging* process to identify and fix the difficulties that almost inevitably arise as a new solution is put in place. The process will involve an emphasis on learning and the use of formative evaluations focused on improving strategies in practices, programs, projects, and ongoing operations (Patton, 2008).

- Include summative evaluations (Fitzpatrick, Sanders, & Worthen, 2004; Mattesssich, 2003; Patton, 2008) to find out whether strategic goals have actually been achieved once strategies are fully implemented. Summative evaluations (as well as logic models) often differentiate between outputs and outcomes. *Outputs* are the actual actions, behaviors, products, services, or other direct consequences produced by policy changes. *Outcomes* are the benefits of the outputs for stakeholders and the larger meaning attached to those outputs. Outputs, in other words, are substantive changes, whereas outcomes are both substantive improvements and symbolic interpretations. Both are important in determining whether a change has been worth the expenditure of time and effort (McLaughlin & Jordan, 2010).

- Retention of important features of the adopted strategies and plans. As situations change and different actors become involved, implementation can become a kind of *moving target*. It is possible that mutations developed during the course of implementation could do a better job of addressing the issues than the originally adopted strategy or plan can. In general, however, it is more likely that design distortions will subvert avowed strategic aims and gut their intent, so it is important to make sure that important design features are maintained or, if they are not, that the changes are desirable.

- Creation of redesigned organizational (or collaborative or community) arrangements that will ensure long-lasting changes. These new settings are marked by the institutionalization of implicit or explicit principles, norms, rules, decision-making procedures, and incentives; the stabilization of altered patterns of behaviors and attitudes; and the continuation or creation of a coalition of implementers, advocates, and supportive interest groups who favor the changes.

- Establishment or anticipation of review points, during which strategies may be maintained, significantly modified, or terminated. The Strategy Change Cycle is a series of loops, not a straight line. Politics, problems, and desired solutions often change (Kingdon, 2002). There are no once-and-for-all solutions, only temporary victories. Leaders, managers, and planners must be alert to the nature and sources of possible challenges to implemented strategies; they should work to maintain still desirable strategies, to replace strategies with better ones when possible or necessary, and to terminate strategies when their value is low or when they become completely outmoded.

If real public value has been created via these subordinate outcomes, then additional desirable outcomes, such as these, are also likely to be produced:

- Increased support for and legitimization of—or at least no opposition to—the leaders and organizations that have successfully advocated and implemented the changes (Boyne & Chen, 2006; Crosby & Bryson, 2005).

- Individuals involved in effective implementation of desirable changes are likely to experience heightened self-efficacy, self-esteem, and self-confidence (Kelman, 2005; Scharmer, 2009; Schein, 2010).

- Organizations (or collaborations or communities) that effectively implement strategies and plans are likely to enhance their capacities for action in the future. They acquire an expanded repertoire of knowledge, experience, tools, and techniques, and an expanded inventory of intellectual, human, social, political, and civic capital—and therefore are better positioned to undertake and adapt to future changes.

The Implementation Cycle

The Implementation Cycle elaborates Steps 9 and 10 of the Strategy Change Cycle—the steps focused on implementation and reassessment. Alternatively, it may be viewed as a subcycle within the Strategy Change Cycle. The Implementation Cycle consists of five major functions needing to be fulfilled, or categories of action needing to be taken, in order for successful implementation to occur (see Figure 4). These action categories include:

- Understanding implementation and assessing readiness
- Getting organized
- Clarifying strategic and operational directions
- Resourcing and structuring implementation, alignment, and ongoing learning
- Maintaining, changing, or terminating strategies

FIGURE 4

The Implementation Cycle as an Elaboration of Steps 9 and 10 of the Strategy Change Cycle

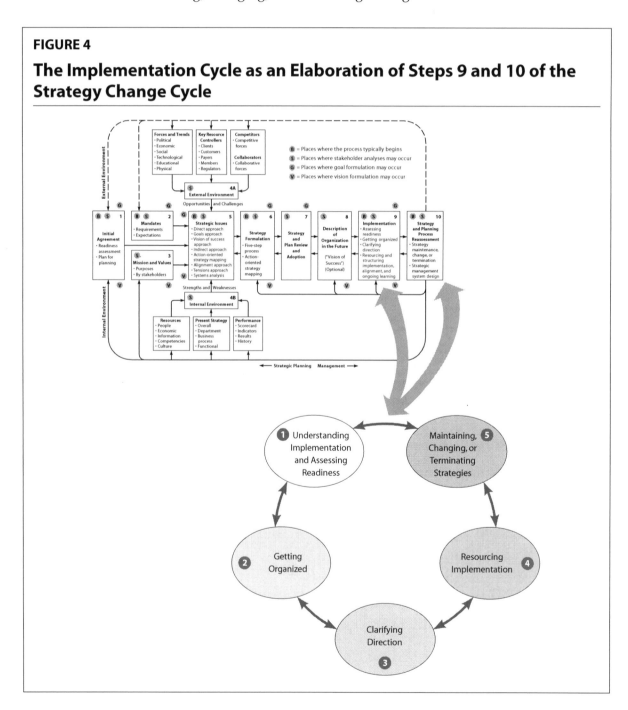

There are three main differences between the Implementation Cycle and the Strategy Change Cycle. First, much more is *given* during implementation. For example, important features of mission, mandates, vision, basic strategies, and basic starting resource allocations are essentially already decided. Although adjustments can be made in these elements, they typically occur on the margin, at least early in the implementation process. Later, as implementation experience increases, key stakeholders may decide to make significant changes in these elements. Second, much more implementation *detail* is developed and added. Strategic plans typically are fairly high-level documents. In contrast, successful implementation requires that high-level concepts be brought to life on the ground. The nitty-gritty operational details matter. This workbook and the worksheets within it are designed to help implementers move higher-level abstractions to grounded action. And finally, typically, the implementers are different from the strategic planners, at least in midsize to large organizations. The planners tend to be higher in the organization's hierarchy, whereas the implementers are closer to the front lines.

The Implementation Cycle's five broad action categories may be broken down into twelve steps (Figure 5). Implementation is viewed as a *cycle* for several reasons. First, the steps are iterative and conclusions reached in one step may be revised based on what is learned in subsequent steps. Second, the process takes place within, and must somehow accommodate, a number of other cyclic phenomena: fiscal years, election cycles, changing fashions, and so on. Finally, all strategies typically run their course and must be rethought; mission, vision, and values may need to be rethought at the same time. A new round of the Strategy Change Cycle is therefore required. The Implementation Cycle's action categories and steps are introduced further in the following paragraphs.

Understanding Implementation and Assessing Readiness

STEP 1: Understanding implementation and assessing readiness. Successful implementation involves effectively aligning actions with aspirations. Earlier we noted that if strategies have been formulated with a clear understanding of what it will take to implement them, and if the strategy formulators and implementers overlap to a significant degree, then implementation is likely to go much more smoothly and quickly. Frequently, however, strategies have been developed without a clear view of implementation requirements, and the strategy formulators and implementers are not the same. In these circumstances a useful starting point for implementers and implementation process overseers is to familiarize themselves with the basics of implementation and to assess the readiness of the organization for implementation work. If the assessment indicates areas for improvement, then work should be directed toward increasing readiness for implementation; otherwise, the chances of implementation success decrease in accord with the lack of readiness.

FIGURE 5
The Implementation Cycle

The implementation process is cyclic. It typically begins after new strategies or strategic plans are adopted (but also sometimes as they are emerging without having been formally adopted) and starts again when strategies are replaced or terminated or a new strategic plan is adopted.

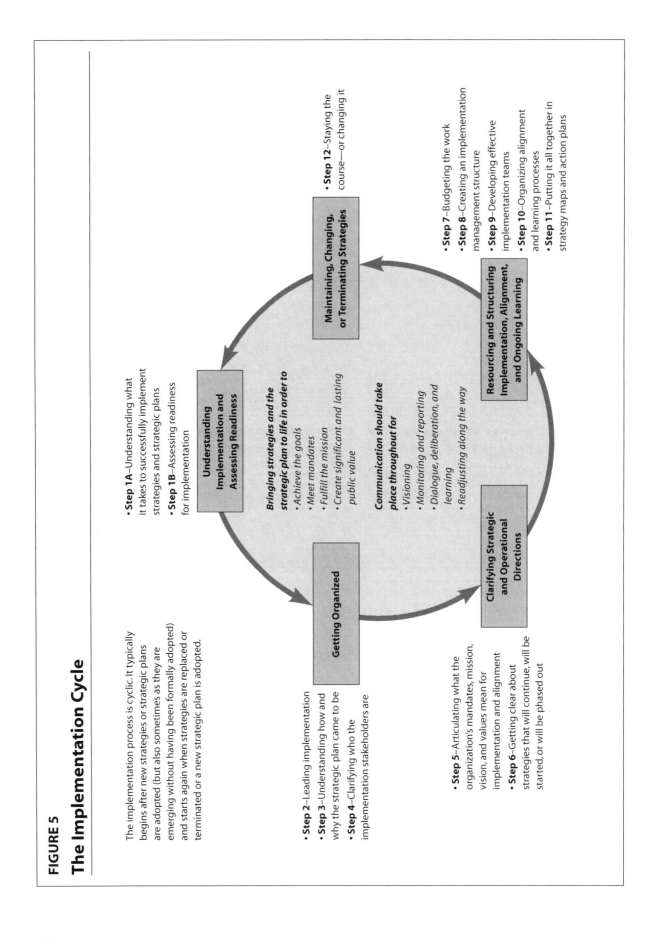

Understanding Implementation and Assessing Readiness

- **Step 1A**–Understanding what it takes to successfully implement strategies and strategic plans
- **Step 1B**–Assessing readiness for implementation

Bringing strategies and the strategic plan to life in order to
- *Achieve the goals*
- *Meet mandates*
- *Fulfill the mission*
- *Create significant and lasting public value*

Communication should take place throughout for
- *Visioning*
- *Monitoring and reporting*
- *Dialogue, deliberation, and learning*
- *Readjusting along the way*

Getting Organized

- **Step 2**–Leading implementation
- **Step 3**–Understanding how and why the strategic plan came to be
- **Step 4**–Clarifying who the implementation stakeholders are

Clarifying Strategic and Operational Directions

- **Step 5**–Articulating what the organization's mandates, mission, vision, and values mean for implementation and alignment
- **Step 6**–Getting clear about strategies that will continue, will be started, or will be phased out

Maintaining, Changing, or Terminating Strategies

- **Step 12**–Staying the course—or changing it

Resourcing and Structuring Implementation, Alignment, and Ongoing Learning

- **Step 7**–Budgeting the work
- **Step 8**–Creating an implementation management structure
- **Step 9**–Developing effective implementation teams
- **Step 10**–Organizing alignment and learning processes
- **Step 11**–Putting it all together in strategy maps and action plans

Getting Organized

STEP 2: Leading implementation. This is the one absolutely crucial requirement. Strategy implementation does not happen without effective leadership of many kinds. Sponsors, champions, facilitators, team leaders, negotiators, and not least, good followers are all required. The purpose of this step is to ensure that the necessary leadership and followership are in place when and where they are needed. It is also important to view implementation as an opportunity for leadership development, thereby preparing people and the organization for sustained strategic management and the next round of strategic planning.

STEP 3: Understanding how and why the strategic plan came to be. Strategic plans are best viewed not as stand-alone objects but as negotiated documents embedded in the contexts and stakeholder relationships that produced them. Strategic plans typically represent explicit and implicit agreements and understandings about what will remain the same about the context and relationships and what will change. Successful implementation depends on understanding what the planners and decision makers saw as worth preserving, on the one hand, and in need of change, on the other hand. Implementers should understand the basic *theory of change* stated or implied by the strategic plan, however unsophisticated it might be. In other words, what are the elements of the plan and their interconnections, and is it reasonable to believe that *if* the strategies and actions outlined are taken, *then* the goals will be achieved, the mission fulfilled, and the mandates met? Special attention needs to be devoted to the organization's culture, what's good about it, and what will need to change, because every significant strategy change also typically involves a cultural change. In short, implementers should understand the reasons why the strategic plan was produced, and how, along with the strengths and weaknesses of the plan and planning process. Implementers also need to realize that successfully implementing a strategic plan can be much more difficult than developing the plan was in the first place.

STEP 4: Clarifying who the implementation stakeholders are. The key to success for both strategic planning and implementation is the satisfaction of key stakeholders according to their criteria for satisfaction. This step is meant to help implementers understand clearly and in detail what the stakeholder environment is for implementation and to plan how and in what ways stakeholders should be engaged in implementation efforts.

Clarifying Strategic and Operational Directions

STEP 5: Articulating what the organization's mission, mandates, and values mean for implementation and alignment. Strategies should help the organization meet its mandates, fulfill its mission, and realize its vision and values. Implementers should explore what the mandates, mission, and values mean or imply for implementing the strategies. For example, if the organization has adopted a set of guiding values, presumably they should be reflected in the implementation process, its outputs, and outcomes. If not, something probably should change about the implementation or about the values.

STEP 6: **Getting clear about strategies that will continue, will be started, or will be phased out.** Strategies are defined as the patterns across policies, goals, actions, budgets, and other implementation elements. Unfortunately, existing strategies and the strategies outlined in strategic plans are typically rather vague. In this step implementers flesh out what existing strategies and any new ones articulated in the strategic plan mean in practice. This may involve (1) clarifying each strategy's *logic model* (Knowlton & Phillips, 2008; McLaughlin & Jordon, 2010), along with its implied requirements for personnel, competencies, systems, procedures, resources, and so forth; (2) identifying major implementation alternatives, along with the criteria for choosing among them; (3) comparing proposed strategies with existing strategies and deciding what to do as a result of the comparison, that is, drop one or the other, merge strategies, or somehow differentiate among them; (4) identifying implications for needed competencies and distinctive competencies and assets; (5) identifying cultural implications of strategy alternatives; and finally (6) developing performance indicators for each strategy.

Resourcing and Structuring Implementation, Alignment, and Ongoing Learning

STEP 7: **Budgeting the work.** An effort should have been made during the strategic planning process to separate strategic from operational concerns. Strategic matters should have been dealt with by senior leaders and other key stakeholders and perhaps a strategic planning coordinating committee, and operational matters referred to an operations group. During implementation, strategic and operational concerns must in effect be brought back together and reintegrated. Effective strategy implementation depends on having realistic financial, staff, staff development, technology, time, and other resource budgets available to reconcile the new strategies the plan calls for with ongoing strategies; it also depends on having a clear agenda of what will no longer be done—the *stop agenda*—owing to inadequate resources. This is the step where that should happen, unless the work was already done as part of developing the strategic plan. Attention to the development of a stop agenda is particularly important, so that freed resources can be devoted to higher priority uses.

STEP 8: **Creating an implementation management structure.** Many strategic initiatives should be treated as programs or projects (or portfolios of programs and projects) requiring special implementation management structures. This step assists implementers to design, organize, and staff these structures and also figure out how they might best be managed to support implementation.

STEP 9: Developing effective implementation teams. Teams are a basic implementation vehicle, and attention should be devoted to how they are assembled and led and how they function. Meetings are an important aspect of teamwork and they should be managed effectively. A great team can do almost anything; a badly organized, managed, and functioning team can be worse than useless.

STEP 10: Organizing alignment and learning processes. An important key to successful implementation is a well-designed learning process so that midcourse corrections are made along the way; alignments within and across strategies and structures are made; new learning is transferred to additional places where it is needed; and the organization, its members, and involved stakeholders acquire enhanced capacity for creating lasting public value and the next round of strategy change. The purpose of this step therefore is to put in place a process and mechanisms for ensuring ongoing learning to improve implementation, increase organizational alignment, and build capacity for useful work in the future. There are two keys: having an adequate performance control system in place in order to monitor and improve performance, and creating a system of interactive meetings to discuss performance and outline necessary actions to improve it. Getting the timing right for performance control and improvement activities is important, so that needed reviews and changes mesh with decision making.

STEP 11: Putting it all together in strategy maps and action plans. Effectively implementing strategies involves pulling together information garnered in previous steps into strategy maps and action plans. Strategy maps are word-and-arrow (or statement-and-arrow) diagrams that show how mission and vision may be achieved via particular goals, and how the goals may be achieved by pursuing specific strategies. The maps make graphic the logic that guides the strategic plan and its implementation. They offer a big-picture view that helps implementers all be—quite literally—on the same page. They help implementers see the forest and the individual trees. Action plans provide the detailed guidance on how to implement specific strategies within given time frames.

Maintaining, Replacing, or Terminating Strategies

STEP 12: Staying the course—or changing it. The final step of the Implementation Cycle is essentially the same as the final step of the Strategy Change Cycle (reassess strategies and the strategic planning process). Implemented strategies are reviewed to find out what worked, what did not work, and why. Judgments are made about which strategies should be kept as is, which should be modified, and which should be ended. The review may be extended to assess the strategic planning process as well and to set the stage for the next round of strategic planning.

The Implementation Cycle: Theory Versus Practice

Although the implementation process has been laid out in a linear, sequential manner, it must be emphasized that in practice the process is typically iterative: participants usually rethink what they have done several times before they reach final decisions represented in strategy maps and action plans. Moreover, the process does not always begin at the beginning. After implementation has begun, organizations may find themselves confronted with difficulties that lead them to engage in a serious review and analysis of how to improve the implementation process.

It is also important to note that implementation efforts must be tailored to the context in which they take place, including fitting with or within ongoing processes of organizational operation and change (processes that are typically cyclical or nonlinear). As noted, these processes include budgeting cycles, legislative cycles, decision-making routines of the governing board, and other change initiatives.

There are also different levels of implementation guidance and control, ranging from the more abstract or conceptual (such as mission, vision, and general goals) to the more specific or concrete (such as budgets and individual work plans). Implementation efforts may be orchestrated from the top, proceeding *deductively* down to the more concrete and specific level, or may be undertaken at the more concrete level, rising *inductively* toward the more abstract or conceptual level. Most often, implementation involves a combination of deductive and inductive approaches, and these must be blended as wisely as possible (Hill & Hupe, 2009; Mintzberg, Ahlstrand, & Lampel, 2009). This workbook is designed to accommodate top-down and bottom-up, deductive and inductive, implementation processes.

Key Design Choices

A number of interconnected design choices must be made to enhance the prospects for successful implementation. Here are some of the more important choices (also see Worksheet 3):

- What are the purposes of the implementation effort?

    In what ways are implementation efforts intended to enhance organizational or community performance and create public value?

    What other outcomes or benefits of implementation are being or should be sought?

    What values should the implementation process embody in the way it is organized and pursued?

- Whose implementation effort is it?

  Whose effort does it need to be in order to be successful?

  Is implementation to be owned by a community, collaboration, organization, organizational unit, program, project, or function?

  Is there a coalition in support of implementing desired changes? If so, who are the coalition members?

  How will the coalition be maintained?

  If a supportive coalition does not exist, how will it be built?

  What are the implications of this choice for participation?

- How will or should the process be tailored to the situation at hand?

  What are the implications of prior successful and unsuccessful implementation efforts for what comes next?

  Are new goal formulation and visioning activities necessary, and if so, where and when will they occur in the process?

  How will implementation efforts fit with other ongoing organizational processes and change efforts, such as budgeting cycles, process improvement and information technology initiatives, and so forth?

  How will the process be tailored to fit the organization's culture—even if that culture needs to be changed in some ways?

- How will or should the process be managed?

  Who are or should be the key sponsors of the process?

  Who will or should champion and manage the process? Who will or should champion important initiatives?

  How will or should the implementation process be broken down into programs, projects, phases, activities, tasks, and so on?

  What is or should be the time frame for implementation and its constituent parts?

  What kind of participation processes will be needed?

  What kinds of commitments will be required from sponsors and implementers in terms of time, energy, and financial and political resources?

  How will the process foster ongoing learning and midcourse corrections?

- What are the requirements for success?

  How will success be measured?

  What should or must happen in terms of key organizational performance indicators?

Who must be a part of the guiding coalition?

What is necessary for the process to be seen as legitimate in terms of procedure, process, support, and content?

What is it about the culture that must be honored? What has to change?

What organizational knowledge, skills, and competencies are required for implementation to succeed?

What are the absolute minimum resource requirements, in terms of funds, people, support, and other resources, without which the implementation is doomed to fail? (Recall that management attention is likely to be the most crucial resource.)

What Are the Dangers to Avoid?

There are many ways in which implementation can fail. Without broad and supportive sponsorship, a strong guiding coalition, careful and skilled management, adequate resources, necessary competence across the board, excellent meshing with ongoing processes, good timing, and a fair measure of luck, implementation may fail. The challenge is not so much with existing strategies that will be maintained; it is more with existing strategies that need substantial modification, new strategies just starting, and especially strategies that have been targeted for elimination. Whenever you ask people to do something differently, you may threaten the organization's existing culture, coalitions, values, structures, processes, and interaction patterns. Frustration, anger, rage, and rejection of the process may result, no matter how necessary the changes may be to ensure organizational survival and prosperity. There is also often an inherent skepticism and resistance to change among line managers, who have a strong operational orientation and want to know how change will improve their work situations. Fortunately, there are likely to be stakeholders dissatisfied with the status quo and able and willing to take on the new challenges. Tapping their disquiet, enthusiasm for change, and skill provides important resources for implementation (Kelman, 2005).

What Are the Keys to a Successful Process?

In many ways the keys to success are the mirror image of the potential sources of failure:

Be sure the organization is ready. Conduct a readiness assessment. The organization needs to be prepared to engage in successful implementation. If the organization is not prepared, identify capacity problems and figure out how to remedy them. Use the Readiness Assessment Questionnaire (Worksheet 2) to assist you in determining whether your organization is ready for implementation.

Strengthen leadership and ensure adequate participation by key stakeholders. You will need strong process sponsors and champions and the support of key stakeholders throughout the implementation process. Make sure they are willing to devote the time needed to ensure implementation success.

Make sure important initiatives are overseen by a skillful champion (or champions). Sponsors provide the authority and power to initiate, carry out, and legitimize implementation efforts. But sponsors are typically not involved in managing the process on a day-to-day basis—the champion is. You need a champion who understands what needs to be done and is committed to it.

Make sure you have adequate management capacity for effective implementation. Implementation doesn't just happen—in addition to sponsors and champions, adequate management capacity is needed to bring strategies to life. Commit the management resources necessary for a successful effort, including drawing on people who are skilled at implementation.

Build understanding to support wise implementation with thoughtful communication, action, and ongoing learning. Clearly communicate the purposes of the implementation process to key stakeholders. Engage in the dialogue and deliberation necessary to build adequate understanding of what is to be implemented, why, and how. Manage expectations so that neither too much nor too little is expected of the implementation process. Take the time and allocate the resources to "do it right."

Cultivate necessary political support. Sponsorship by key decision makers is typically crucial to the success of implementation efforts. They must be willing to emphasize the importance of the efforts and to intervene as necessary to respond to circumstances and keep things on track. Beyond that, a coalition of supporters must be built that is large enough and strong enough to adopt the strategic plan and support it during implementation.

Foster effective decision making for implementation. Help decision makers focus on ensuring successful implementation. Develop an implementation process and action planning efforts that will ensure the realization of adopted strategies by linking these processes to operational plans and to resource allocation decisions. Build in effective mechanisms for conflict management, because conflict will certainly occur— it's a natural and expected part of any change effort.

Make sure you have adequate resources—including necessary competencies—for successful implementation. Management capacity is the resource typically in shortest supply, but other resources are also crucial. These include adequate funding, staffing, space, transportation, orientation and training, technology, time, and possibly many other kinds of resources. Competency to do the job is a fundamental element of success. A poverty resource budget can be a death sentence. If you do not have adequate resources, figure out what you can do about it, if anything.

Design a process that is likely to succeed. Build on existing organizational and management change efforts and routines. Fit the implementation process to the situation at hand, which may mean pursuing either direct or some sort of staged implementation. Fit the process to the organization's (or collaboration's or community's) culture. Link the process to key decision-making processes and include ways to manage conflicts that arise. Be realistic about the scope and scale of the implementation effort in light of the management capacity and resources available. Find a way to accommodate the day-to-day demands on people's time while also asking them to do new things. Make sure that people see implementation as genuinely helpful.

Implementation Purposes and the Implementation Cycle

Figure 6 presents a somewhat finer grained view of the Implementation Cycle than the one found in Figure 5. Figure 6 shows how the steps of the Implementation Cycle are designed to help an organization fulfill five functions (or broad categories of action) meant to create desired implementation outcomes. The overall purpose of implementation (and strategic management) is to create significant and lasting public value, chiefly through helping the organization fulfill its mission, meet its mandates, and achieve its goals. Achieving these purposes requires implementing the organization's strategies and strategic plan—and perhaps revising them as needed along the way. Effective implementation depends on these five key, interconnected functions (or categories of action) being performed well: understanding implementation and assessing readiness; getting organized; clarifying strategic and operational directions and details; resourcing and structuring implementation, alignment, and ongoing learning; and maintaining, replacing, or terminating strategies. The twelve steps of the Implementation Cycle, other process design features, and the actions they foster are designed to fulfill these functions and thereby create the desired outcomes. Most steps contribute to more than one function, or broad category of action, and therefore the whole process must be seen as interactive. Planned and as-needed dialogue and deliberation are necessary throughout the process to make sure necessary things occur in the right way at the right time in the right place to produce significant and lasting public value.

Worksheet Directions

1. Consider using Worksheet 1 to interview those involved in developing or adopting the strategic plan, in order to gain important information about the planners' and adopters' intentions and views; this information may have a significant impact on the implementation process.

FIGURE 6

Implementation Purposes, Categories of Action, Design Features, and Context

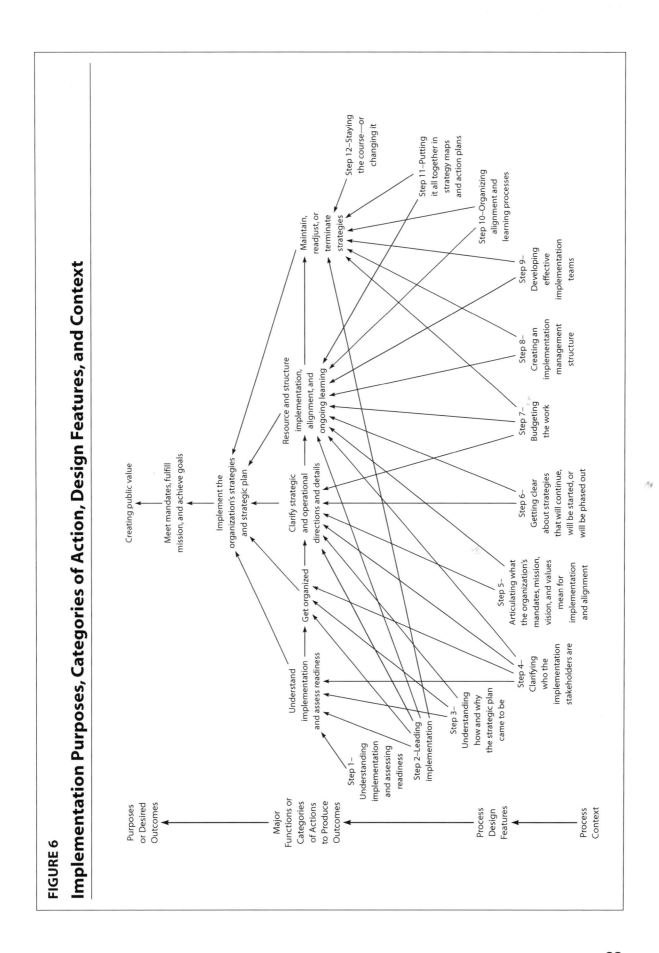

2. A summary of responses to the interviews should be put together and shared with key decision makers and others who can affect the shape and content of the implementation process.

3. Consider as well using the Implementation Readiness Assessment Questionnaire (Worksheet 2) to understand how prepared the organization is to implement its strategic plan. Implementation sponsors, champions, and key stakeholders are likely respondents.

4. A summary of responses to the questionnaire should be compiled and key decision makers should discuss what the results mean. Should implementation efforts move full steam ahead, or should efforts first be made to address any issues that come up as a result of the assessment?

5. Those involved in guiding initial implementation efforts should then work individually to fill out Worksheet 3, "Key Implementation Design Choices," and then they should discuss the resulting opinions as a group. Early on in the implementation effort, answers to many of the questions are likely to be unclear. This worksheet should therefore be updated as new information becomes available and subsequent steps in the Implementation Cycle are completed.

WORKSHEET 1

Interviewing People About the Upcoming Implementation Process

Instructions. Those thinking about implementing a strategic plan should consider interviewing key decision makers and other internal and external stakeholders who were involved in developing and adopting the strategic plan. The interviews may be very helpful in building support for implementation and making sure the process is designed in such a way that it will be successful.

Consider interviewing those who might have an interest in sponsoring, championing, or otherwise leading the implementation effort; and those who would most affect or be affected by the effort. Group interviews may also be useful but will need to be effectively facilitated and an adequate record kept of ideas offered and conclusions reached. Group interviews can be a part of targeted outreach and communications programs designed to build support for implementation.

Some preliminary stakeholder analysis may be necessary in order to develop the appropriate list of people or groups to be interviewed. After the interviewee list is decided upon, those exploring how best to pursue implementation should do the interviewing. It may be wise to have two interviewers conduct each interview—to understand more clearly what is being said and not said, to improve note-taking accuracy, and to broaden understanding of the implications for planning process design.

Consider using the following list of questions as a guide. Ask the person being interviewed to answer the questions from his or her perspective, not from that of the organization as a whole. To promote candor, emphasize that all interviews will be kept confidential; and to promote participation, note that summary information will be made available in the future.

Interview as Part of Readiness Assessment for Implementation

Date:_____

Name of interviewer(s):_____

Interviewee's (or group's) name:_____

Organization unit:_____ Function:_____

Job title:_____

Contact information:_____

External stakeholder name:_____ Title:_____

Contact information:_____

1. What do you think the most important reasons were for undertaking a strategic planning effort? Why do you think so?

Reasons for Engaging in Strategic Planning	Can You Say More About That?

Worksheet 1

2. What were the major substantive and process issues that needed to be addressed as part of the process? (Answers to this question may have been covered by answers to the prior question.)

Substantive Issues (need to improve client satisfaction, need to address funding shortages, and so on)	Process Issues (need to ensure adequate participation, need for reasonable transparency, need to improve quality of decision making, and so on)

Worksheet 1

Implementing and Sustaining Your Strategic Plan.

3. What do you think were the most important outcomes of the strategic planning process, both in terms of *tangible* products—such as a strategic plan or changes in resource allocations, behaviors, or facilities—and *intangible* products—such as changed understandings, relationships, or organizational reputation?

4. Were there any issues not addressed as part of the strategic planning process that should have been addressed?

5. Does the fact that those issues were not addressed have any implications for implementation of the strategic plan?

6. What do think the top 5 priorities for implementation ought to be? Please rank them from 1 to 5 with 1 being the most important.

   1.

   2.

   3.

   4.

   5.

7. Should they be addressed in that order, or not?

8. What do you think needs to stay the same or endure as a result of the implementation process, and what should change?

Stay the Same	Change

Worksheet 1

9. For the implementation effort to succeed, what do you think must happen? In other words, what do you think is absolutely necessary for success? Why do you think so?

Required for Strategic Planning Success	Why Is It a Requirement?

10. Who should have a leadership role in the implementation process and why? Who should probably not have a role in the process and why?

Should Have Some Leadership Role	Should Probably Not Have a Leadership Role

Worksheet 1

Implementing and Sustaining Your Strategic Plan.

11. Can you think of any key questions that this worksheet has not touched on?

12. Do you have any other insights, ideas, or suggestions regarding strategic planning for this organization?

Thank you for your time!

Worksheet 1

Implementing and Sustaining Your Strategic Plan.

WORKSHEET 2

Implementation Readiness Assessment Questionnaire

Instructions. This questionnaire is meant to help those thinking ahead to the process of implementing a strategic plan. Implementation can be very challenging work and an organization needs to be ready for it. Being "ready" doesn't mean everything must be in fabulous shape; it does mean having a good idea of the current situation and what might be done over the course of an implementation process to increase the chances of success. The questionnaire provides a template that should be adapted as needed to make it useful.

Implementation Readiness Assessment Questionnaire

Dear _____,

   We will soon have a new strategic plan and must prepare ourselves for implementation efforts in accord with the plan. Implementation will include continuing many of the things we already do, integrating new initiatives into ongoing operations, and phasing out other activities. The purpose of this Implementation Readiness Assessment Questionnaire is to take stock of where we are now and what we might need to do to prepare ourselves for successful implementation.

Please complete the following information:

Name: _____

My unit, division, or organization is: _____

My program, project, or functional area is: _____

Instructions for Completing the Questionnaire

There are no "right" or "wrong" answers.

For each statement in this questionnaire, please *check* the box for the number from 1 (strongly disagree) to 5 (strongly agree) that best reflects your response to the statement. When a statement or set of statements does not apply to your situation, please mark the NA (not applicable) box.

Please be candid in your responses and draw on your experiences in the last two years.

There is a space for comments after each set of questions.

Understanding implementation (Step 1)	1 Strongly Disagree	2 Disagree	3 Neither Agree nor Disagree	4 Agree	5 Strongly Agree	NA
We have extensive experience with successfully implementing changes—we understand what is involved and how to make it work.						
We make regular dialogue and deliberation a part of everything we do.						
We routinely set time aside to assess what is working well, what is not, what modifications might improve what we do, and what lessons we should take away for current and future use.						

Comments:

Worksheet 2

Implementing and Sustaining Your Strategic Plan.

Leading implementation (Step 2)	1 Strongly Disagree	2 Disagree	3 Neither Agree nor Disagree	4 Agree	5 Strongly Agree	NA
We have a strong sponsor(s) to authorize and legitimize the implementation effort.						
We have a strong champion(s) in place to oversee day-to-day implementation efforts.						
Our leadership team is clearly focused—our goal is clear.						
There is a high level of trust among the members of the leadership team—our communications are open and honest.						
I personally have a strong sense of urgency to move our organization ahead.						

Comments:

Worksheet 2

Implementing and Sustaining Your Strategic Plan.

Understanding how and why the strategic plan came to be (Step 3)	1 Strongly Disagree	2 Disagree	3 Neither Agree nor Disagree	4 Agree	5 Strongly Agree	NA
We understand clearly why the strategic planning effort was undertaken, which issues were addressed, which were not, and what tangible and intangible immediate outputs and outcomes were produced.						
We understand what those involved in the strategic planning process think are the requirements for imple-mentation success.						
We understand what goes on when the organization works and succeeds—and what goes on when things are not working well.						

Comments:

Worksheet 2

Implementing and Sustaining Your Strategic Plan.

Clarifying who the implementation stakeholders are (Step 4)	1 Strongly Disagree	2 Disagree	3 Neither Agree nor Disagree	4 Agree	5 Strongly Agree	NA
We know who our key stakeholders are and what matters to them.						
We engage with key stakeholders in effective ways to facilitate our work.						
We have a strong coalition in place to support and protect implementation efforts.						

Comments:

Worksheet 2

Implementing and Sustaining Your Strategic Plan.

Articulating what the organization's mandates, mission, vision, and values mean for implementation and alignment (Step 5)	1 Strongly Disagree	2 Disagree	3 Neither Agree nor Disagree	4 Agree	5 Strongly Agree	NA
As an organization (or group) we have a clear mission.						
As an organization all our work is informed by our mission.						
We pay attention to our mission on a day-to-day basis.						
We have a clear and shared vision of organizational success to guide our implementation efforts.						
We know what success would look like for us as an organization.						

Comments:

Worksheet 2

Implementing and Sustaining Your Strategic Plan.
Copyright © 2011 by John Wiley & Sons, Inc. All rights reserved.

Getting clear about strategies that will continue, will be started, or will be phased out (Step 6)	1 Strongly Disagree	2 Disagree	3 Neither Agree nor Disagree	4 Agree	5 Strongly Agree	NA
We are able to do both our day-to-day work and accommodate major changes.						
Risk taking is encouraged in our organization.						

Comments:

Budgeting the work (Step 7)	1 Strongly Disagree	2 Disagree	3 Neither Agree nor Disagree	4 Agree	5 Strongly Agree	NA
We always link our budgets directly to our strategic priorities.						
We always have or find the resources needed to get the job done.						

Comments:

Worksheet 2

Implementing and Sustaining Your Strategic Plan.

Creating an implementation management structure (Step 8)	1 Strongly Disagree	2 Disagree	3 Neither Agree nor Disagree	4 Agree	5 Strongly Agree	NA
We have the needed management capacity (that is, sufficient management staff numbers, time, and attention) to implement the strategies and strategic plan.						
We have the needed management competencies (skills and abilities) to implement the strategies and strategic plan.						
We have effective two-way communications up and down and within and outside the organization.						
We have more than adequate information technology needed to do the work (including appropriate Web 2.0 and higher technologies).						
We are very good at managing programs and projects.						
We finish projects on time and on budget.						
Our organization's structure is flexible to accommodate change.						

Comments:

Worksheet 2

Implementing and Sustaining Your Strategic Plan.
Copyright © 2011 by John Wiley & Sons, Inc. All rights reserved.

Developing effective implementation teams (Step 9)	1 Strongly Disagree	2 Disagree	3 Neither Agree nor Disagree	4 Agree	5 Strongly Agree	NA
There is effective cross-organizational cooperation.						
There are adequate incentives to encourage working together.						
We have excellent conflict management mechanisms and processes in place.						
We work well in teams.						
I feel valued as an employee.						

Comments:

Worksheet 2

Implementing and Sustaining Your Strategic Plan.

Organizing alignment and learning processes (Step 10)	1 Strongly Disagree	2 Disagree	3 Neither Agree nor Disagree	4 Agree	5 Strongly Agree	NA
Deliberation and dialogue about important matters are encouraged in our organization.						
We act quickly to address important issues.						
We make extensive use of data and analysis to make important decisions.						
There is a merit-based system of rewards and recognition tied to goal achievement and working together.						
We have well-understood and accepted performance measures in place against which to assess all of our important work.						
We are a performance-driven organization.						
We make extensive use of formative evaluations and ongoing collective learning processes to constantly improve our work and results.						

Comments:

Worksheet 2

Implementing and Sustaining Your Strategic Plan.

Putting it all together in strategy maps and action plans (Step 11)	1 Strongly Disagree	2 Disagree	3 Neither Agree nor Disagree	4 Agree	5 Strongly Agree	NA
We use clear and easily understood graphics to show the direct connections from mission, mandates, and vision to strategies, actions, and results on the ground.						
Action planning is standard practice in our organization for every initiative, ongoing operation, and individual.						
The contributions of each action plan to the achievement of our strategic goals and mission are clear.						
The board has its own action plan.						

Comments:

Staying the course—or changing it (Step 12)	1 Strongly Disagree	2 Disagree	3 Neither Agree nor Disagree	4 Agree	5 Strongly Agree	NA
We are not afraid to quit doing things that are either low priority or not working well.						
We have a strong work ethic as an organization (or group).						
I am open to change.						

Comments:

Any final thoughts?

Worksheet 2

Implementing and Sustaining Your Strategic Plan.

WORKSHEET 3
Key Implementation Design Choices

Instructions. A number of interconnected design choices must be made to enhance the prospects for successful implementation. The questions listed in this worksheet are designed to help the initiators of the implementation effort explore these choices and to set the stage for further discussions on implementation readiness and the design of the process. This information will be aggregated, and individual comments will be kept confidential. At the outset of the implementation effort, answers to many of these questions are likely to be unclear. This worksheet should therefore be updated as new information becomes available.

Name: _____

Organizational unit (if you are an external respondent, please note that here):

_____

Job title: _____

1. What are the purposes of the new implementation effort from your perspective?

    a. In what ways are the implementation efforts intended to enhance organizational or community performance and create public value?

b. What other outcomes or benefits of implementation are being or should be sought?

c. What values should the implementation process embody in the way it is organized and pursued?

2. Whose implementation effort is this currently (for example, the board, management, some other group or person)?

a. Whose effort does it need to be in order to be successful?

b. Is the implementation going to be "owned"—ultimately, if not now—by a community, collaboration, organization, organizational unit, program, project, or function? If yes, who or what is that "owner"?

c. Is there a coalition in support of implementing desired changes? If so, who makes up that coalition?

d. How will the coalition be maintained?

e. If a supportive coalition does not exist, how will it be built?

f. What are the implications of your answers to items a through e for participation?

3. How will or should the implementation process be tailored to the situation at hand?

a. What are the implications of prior successful implementation efforts for what comes next?

b. What are the implications of prior unsuccessful implementation efforts for what comes next?

c. Are new goal formulation and visioning activities necessary, and if so, where and when should they occur in the process?

d. How will implementation efforts fit with other ongoing organizational processes and change efforts, such as budgeting cycles, process improvements, information technology initiatives, and so forth?

e. How will the process be tailored to fit the organization's culture—even if that culture needs to be changed in some ways?

4. How will or should the process be managed?

a. Who are or should be the key sponsors of the process?

b. Who will or should champion and manage the overall process?

c. Who will or should champion important initiatives?

d. How will or should the implementation process be broken down into programs, projects, phases, activities, tasks, and so on?

e. What is or should be the time frame for the implementation process overall and for its major constituent parts?

f. What kind of participation processes will be needed?

g. What kinds of commitments will be required from sponsors and implementers in terms of time, energy, and financial and political resources?

h. How will the process foster ongoing learning and midcourse corrections?

Worksheet 3

Implementing and Sustaining Your Strategic Plan.

5. What are the requirements for success?

    a. How will success be measured?

    b. What should or must happen with the key organizational performance indicators?

    c. Who must be a part of the guiding implementation coalition?

    d. What is needed in terms of procedure, process, support, and content for the process to be seen as legitimate?

Worksheet 3

e. What features of the organization's culture must be honored? What has to change?

f. What organizational knowledge, skills, abilities, and competencies are required for implementation to succeed?

g. What are the absolute minimum resource requirements, in terms of funds, people, support, and other resources, without which implementation is doomed to fail? (Recall that management attention is likely to be the most crucial resource.)

Additional comments:

Worksheet 3

Part 2

Getting Organized

2
Getting Organized

Step 2: Learning implementation

Step 3: Understanding how and why the strategic plan came to be

Step 4: Clarifying who the implementation stakeholders are

Step 2

Leading Implementation

Purpose of Step

Implementation efforts will succeed only when enough people are inspired, mobilized, and guided—that is, led—to make it happen. The purpose of this step is to assist your organization or group to create the leadership group and coalition needed to support, protect, and guide implementation efforts. There is *no* substitute for effective leadership (and committed followership) when it comes to integrating strategic planning with ongoing implementation—that is, engaging in *strategic management*—across an organization to enhance meeting mandates, fulfilling the mission, and in general creating significant and lasting public value. Strategic management provides a set of useful concepts, practices, procedures, and tools designed to help executives, managers, and others with the ongoing work of implementing desirable strategies and strategic plans. In the process, shared ownership of the mission, vision, values, and goals is built and responsibility for performance is often both shared collectively and delegated appropriately. But whether strategic management helps or hurts depends on how formal and informal leaders and followers at all organizational levels use it—or misuse it. This workbook is designed to help those who are committed to effective strategic management make it an organizational reality.

Following Crosby and Bryson (2005), we define leadership as "the inspiration and mobilization of others to undertake collective action in pursuit of the common good" (p. xix). This definition suggests that *leadership* and *leaders* are not the same thing. Effective leadership in and for public and nonprofit organizations, collaborations, and communities is a collective enterprise involving many people playing different leader and follower roles at different times. Indeed, the same people may be leaders at some times and followers at different times over the course of an entire strategy change cycle or specific implementation effort.

This chapter draws extensively on Barbara C. Crosby and J. M. Bryson, *Leadership for the Common Good: Tackling Public Problems in a Shared-Power World*, 2nd ed. (San Francisco: Jossey-Bass/Wiley, 2005).

The following interconnected leadership tasks are important if strategic planning and implementation are to be effective:

- Sponsoring the implementation process
- Championing the process
- Facilitating the process
- Fostering collective leadership
- Using dialogue and deliberation to create a meaningful implementation process; clarify the implications of mandates, mission, and goals for implementation; detail desirable strategies; develop effective action plans; and foster organizational learning
- Making and executing implementation decisions
- Enforcing rules, settling disputes, and managing residual conflicts
- Putting it all together, and preparing for ongoing strategic change

Possible Desired Implementation Outcomes

- Committed implementation process sponsor(s) enlisted
- Able and committed implementation process champion(s) enlisted
- Necessary facilitators and facilitation resources available when needed
- Implementation coordinating committee established
- Needed implementation teams in place
- Necessary and desirable forums established
- Forums linked in effective ways to necessary and desirable arenas
- Rules enforced, disputes settled, and residual conflicts managed well
- Implementation leadership efforts integrated in such a way that real public value is created and the stage is set for the next round of the Strategy Change Cycle

Understanding the Context

Implementation leaders should help affected stakeholders view the implementation of strategies and the strategic plan in the context of relevant social, political, economic, technological, and ecological systems and trends. Understanding the context allows implementers to understand more clearly why they are being called on to continue some strategies, change or add others, and eliminate still others. Stakeholders will thus be helped to see the organization's history as an interweaving of stability and change and of designed interventions adapted to emergent realities. See, for example, Worksheets 18 to 21, 27 to 31, and 42 in *Creating Your Strategic Plan*, third edition (Bryson & Alston, 2011).

Understanding the People Involved, Including Oneself

Understanding oneself and others will help individuals to develop the insight and strength of character that energizes leadership and will increase the chances that strategy implementation efforts will actually succeed. Leaders should seek to understand the strengths and weaknesses of the people who are or should be involved in implementation efforts, including themselves. Finding and placing in key positions those people who have a passion for fulfilling the organization's mission, meeting its mandates, and contributing to the well-being of multiple stakeholders will make for quicker and easier implementation. Yet this passion must be coupled with a degree of humility and open-mindedness if a leader (or follower) is to avoid self-righteousness, rigidity, or hubris (Crosby & Bryson, 2005; Delbecq, 2006). In addition to passion tempered by humility and open-mindedness, other personal strengths to seek in leaders (and followers) include professional or technical competencies, organizational position and savvy, interpersonal skills, self-efficacy, compassion, cultural sensitivity, moral integrity, and courage. A sense of humor and openness to learning are also very helpful. Leaders should remember that understanding and marshaling personal assets is perhaps the most powerful instrument of all (Lipman-Blumen, 1996).

Sponsoring the Implementation Process

Implementation sponsors are typically top positional leaders—and often are the members of a policy board, cabinet, or executive committee acting collectively. They have enough prestige, power, and authority to commit the organization to implementing strategies and the strategic plan and to hold people accountable for carrying out this implementation. Sponsors are not necessarily involved in the day-to-day operational details of implementation—the champions, line managers, and frontline staff do that—but they do establish important features of the implementation context, make choices and commit resources that improve the chances for success, and pay careful attention to implementation progress along the way. They have a vested interest in achieving success and do what they can to make it happen. They also are typically important sources of knowledge about key issues and effective ways of addressing those issues and about the organization and its environment in general. They are likely to be especially knowledgeable about how to fit implementation efforts to key decision points. Finally, when organizations are under pressure to change, some people in the organization are probably quite discontented with the status quo and wanting change but may be prompted to engage in actual change efforts only when a powerful sponsor endorses the changes (Kelman, 2005).

Implementation sponsors should consider the following guidelines (and consider using them as their job description for the implementation process):

1. *Articulate the purpose and importance of the implementation effort.* See Worksheet 10 in Step 3.

2. *Commit necessary resources—time, money, energy, legitimacy—to the effort.* A crucial way of making the process real is through allocating resources to it. Nothing will demonstrate leaders' seriousness (or lack of it) about implementation more than that. See Worksheets 28, 29, and 30 in Step 7.

3. *Emphasize throughout the implementation process that results will be and are being produced that are important to the organization's mission, mandates, and key stakeholders, and that public value will be and is being created.* This is another crucial way of making the implementation process real for participants and getting them to take it seriously and invest the necessary effort. See Worksheets 19 through 23 in Step 5, 24 through 27 in Step 6, and 49 through 56 in Step 11 for possible performance indicators.

4. *Encourage and reward hard work, smart and creative thinking, constructive dialogue, and multiple sources of input and insight aimed at ensuring successful implementation.*

5. *Be aware of the possible need for outside consultants.* Outside consultants may be needed to help with various aspects of the implementation process. It is a sign of strength to ask for help when you need it. Enough money must be budgeted to pay for any consultants you may need.

6. *Be willing to exercise power and authority to keep the process on track.* Implementation efforts can break down in a variety of ways, particularly when people are being asked to do some things differently and the organization's culture and routines are being challenged. Sponsors use their authority to provide continuous support for change until the process builds up enough momentum that desired changes take on a life of their own and become a part of the organization's culture (Kelman, 2005).

Championing the Implementation Process

The champions are the people who have primary responsibility for managing implementation efforts on a day-to-day basis. Most implementation champions will be line managers, but others may play the role effectively as well. They are the ones who keep people on course, keep track of progress, and also pay attention to all the details. They model the kind of behavior they hope to get from other participants: reasoned, diligent, committed, enthusiastic, and good-spirited pursuit of the common good. They are the cheerleaders who, along with the sponsors, keep implementation efforts on track and push, encourage, and coach implementers and other key participants through any difficulties. Champions need strong interpersonal skills, a commitment to getting the work done, and a good feel for how to manage complexity.

Champions should keep the following guidelines in mind (again, perhaps as a job description):

1. *Keep strategy and strategic plan implementation high on people's agendas.* People will need to be reminded and shown on a regular basis that good things can and will happen when implementation is consistently and effectively pursued.

2. *Think about what has to come together (people, information, resources, completed work) at or before key decision points.* Typically implementation is an assembly process in which people, information of various sorts, resources, and various products must come together at specific decision points or junctures for things to progress. The best champions are good at getting the right people in the right places with the right information and resources at the right time for good things to happen. Without this kind of astute and timely assembly, things either do not come together properly or just plain fall apart (Bryson, Crosby, & Bryson, 2009).

3. *Keep rallying participants and pushing the implementation process along.* Depending on what is being implemented, successful strategy implementation can take a few weeks or several years. Champions should keep the faith and push until implementation efforts do succeed, or until it is clear that they will fail and there is no point to continuing. At the same time, it is important to remember that all change efforts are likely to *feel* like failures in the middle. Champions keep pushing to help implementers and the organization move through the failure stage toward success. Rallying the troops will be easier when champions can show some early wins and continued small (and occasionally large) wins along the way (Kelman, 2005; Weick, 1984).

4. *Develop champions throughout the organization.* A champion-in-chief may oversee the entire implementation, but he or she should seek out champions throughout the organization (collaboration, community) to oversee parts of the process—for example, by chairing task forces or working groups. Having multiple champions adds enthusiasm, spreads the work, and makes implementation efforts less vulnerable to the loss of key personnel. Having multiple champions is especially important when implementation involves a collaboration or community (Bardach, 1998; Huxham & Vangen, 2005; Innes & Booher, 2010).

5. *Be sensitive to power differences.* Differences in status, authority, and access to resources are likely to be pronounced in more hierarchical organizations and within inclusive collaborations. Power differences may enhance implementation but may also slow it down via hidden resistance. Engaging all implementers and sharing power can build understanding of and commitment to implementation and increase implementation success by avoiding foot dragging or sabotage.

Facilitating the Implementation Process

Process facilitators are often helpful in moving implementation efforts along, especially when those efforts must be integrated effectively across boundaries of various sorts. Facilitators can help because of their group process and conflict management skills, the attention they can give to structuring and managing group interactions, and the likelihood that they have no stake in the substantive outcomes of the process, particularly if they are outsiders (Schwarz, 2002). The presence of a facilitator means that champions can be free to participate in substantive discussions without having to worry too much about managing group process. A skilled facilitator can also build people's trust, interpersonal skills, conflict management ability, and capacity for learning in a group. Building trust is important because implementers often come from various parts of the organization and have never worked together before. Skilled facilitation usually depends on the establishment of a successful partnership among facilitators, sponsors, and champions. They may form a kind of core group that assists in moving implementation efforts forward.

Implementation facilitators should consider following these guidelines (or this job description):

1. *Know something about the strategies and strategic plan that are being implemented.* Facilitators play a key role in keeping people on track—so they must know something about where those tracks are!

2. *Tailor the facilitation process to the organization and the groups involved.* Facilitators, along with sponsors and champions, are the ones who are in the best position to design the implementation process so that it fits the organization, the organization's circumstances, and the participants. Facilitators must pay careful attention to both the *tasks* of implementation and the *socio-emotional maintenance* of the groups and teams involved in the process.

3. *Convey a sense of humor and enthusiasm for the implementation process and help groups get unstuck.* Sponsors and champions can express humor and enthusiasm for the process, but not in the way that a facilitator can. Implementation can be alternately tension-ridden and boring. Good facilitators can help people manage

the tensions and relieve the boredom. Facilitators also can assist groups in addressing the challenges they confront over the course of implementation. Facilitators can aid groups in getting unstuck by helping them reframe their situations, invent new options, manage conflict constructively, and tap hidden sources of courage, hope, and optimism (Seligman, 1998; Schwarz, 2002; Bolman & Deal, 2008; Innes & Booher, 2010).

4. *Ensure that participants rather than the facilitators are doing the work.* Skilled facilitators give participants many chances to interact in small groups and to engage each other in dealing with any challenges.

5. *Press groups toward action and the assignment of responsibility for specific actions.* Part of keeping implementation on track is making sure that participants engage in timely action. Pushing people toward action does raise the danger of inducing premature closure, but a good facilitator will have an intuitive sense about when to push for action and when to hold back. He or she will also be good at probing people and groups about the merits of options and the advisability of taking specific actions.

6. *Celebrate success and congratulate people whenever possible.* Facilitators are in an especially good position to communicate success as it happens and to congratulate people and say good things about them in a genuine and natural way.

Fostering Collective Leadership (and Followership)

When strategic planning is successful for public organizations, it is a collective achievement. Many people contribute to its success, sometimes by leading, other times by following. Collective leadership may be fostered through the following approaches:

1. *Consider creating an implementation coordinating committee.* If implementation will involve connecting and coordinating structures, processes, resources, or activities across organizational boundaries, an implementation coordinating committee (ICC) may be useful. The ICC can provide a place and process for arranging assembly of the necessary implementation structures, processes, resources, and activities in such a way that efforts across boundaries are coordinated effectively and conflicts and difficulties are managed satisfactorily. The ICC will provide a crucial focal point for implementation-related discussions and a venue where difficulties can be worked out in reasonable, amicable ways out of the limelight.

2. *Rely on implementation teams.* The team is a basic vehicle for furthering implementation. Champions, in particular, will find they spend much of their

time making sure implementation teams or task forces perform well and make effective contributions to the implementation process. Teams are particularly important for pulling together necessary knowledge about what needs to be done and for building support across boundaries of many kinds. Team leaders naturally must focus on the accomplishment of team goals or tasks, but they also must attend to individual team members' needs and consciously promote group cohesion (Johnson & Johnson, 2008). Team leadership balances direction, mentoring, and facilitation so that everyone can make useful contributions.

Leaders should help team members to

- Communicate effectively face to face and at a distance (this involves promotion of active listening, dialogue, and other conflict management methods)

- Balance unity around a shared purpose with diversity of views and skills

- Define a team mission, goals, norms, and roles

- Adopt or develop and use performance indicators tied to the task at hand

- Establish an atmosphere of trust

- Foster group creativity, continuous learning, and sound decision making

- Obtain necessary resources

- Develop leadership and followership competencies

- Celebrate achievement and overcome adversity

Although it is the role of team leader that typically receives all the attention in books like this, we want to highlight follower roles as well. Active, committed followers play vital roles in keeping leaders on track and in check, contributing knowledge and ideas, promoting change, and carrying out and shaping agreed-upon tasks (Riggio, Chaleff, & Lipman-Blumen, 2008). See Step 9 for more on implementation teams and related worksheets.

3. *Focus on network and coalition development.* Coalitions form as people organize around ideas and interests that allow them to see that they can achieve together what they could not achieve separately. Work to maintain the coalition that adopted the strategies and strategic plan or else develop the new coalition that is needed to support and protect implementation efforts. The way implementation is framed will structure how stakeholders interpret their interests, how they assess the costs and benefits of joining a coalition, and the form and content of winning and losing arguments. Therefore leaders should use the insights gained from the various stakeholder analysis exercises in Step 4 to gain a sense of where stakeholders' interests overlap and how goals, visions, and strategies might be framed to draw significant support from key implementation stakeholders. Typically, every member of a coalition will not

agree on everything, and that is OK. Public leaders should also build a sense of community—meaning a sense of relationship, mutual empowerment, and common purpose—within and beyond their organizations. This is desirable because so many of the problems public and nonprofit organizations are called on to address require collaborative or community responses (Chrislip, 2002; Linden, 2002).

4. *Make leadership and follower development an explicit strategy.* Many organizations invest in leadership development but may not directly tie leadership development to the organization's strategy implementation and change processes.

5. *Establish specific mechanisms for sharing power, responsibility, and accountability.* Authority typically is not shared by policymaking bodies or chief executives because it cannot be by law. But typically power, responsibility, and accountability can be shared, which fosters participation, information and resource sharing, and commitment to plans and strategies and their implementation (Linden, 2002). The use of implementation teams and task forces is a standard means of sharing power. Action plans should spread out responsibilities while also establishing clear accountability.

Using Dialogue and Deliberation to Create a Meaningful Implementation Process

Creating and communicating meaning is the work of visionary leadership and involves helping people to understand and shape what is required during implementation. A vision of success may have been prepared during the strategic planning process. This vision can be an important resource for shaping and guiding meaning making during implementation. But even if there is a preexisting vision of success, the implementation process typically requires ongoing visioning efforts that aid implementers in clearly conceptualizing what they are trying to do and how they should do it, as well as in seeing what progress they are making toward achieving what is typically an increasingly refined vision of what success would look like. Vision is thus more a *verb* than a *noun*. Leaders help people make sense of their experience, and leaders also offer guidance for coping with the present and the future by answering the questions: What's going on here? Where are we heading? What traditions should we preserve as we go? And how will things look when we get there? They frame and shape the perceived context for action, and they manage important stakeholders' perceptions of the organization, its strategies, and their effects (Boal & Schultz, 2007; Neustadt, 1990). In order to facilitate implementation, especially when it involves major changes, they become skilled in the following methods of creating and communicating new meanings:

1. *Understand the design and use of forums.* Forums are the basic settings we humans use to create shared meaning through dialogue and deliberation (Crosby & Bryson, 2005). Much of the work of implementation takes place in forums, where implementers can engage in a fairly uncensored consideration of ideas and views prior to any actual actions being taken. The tasks of sponsoring, championing, and facilitating implementation are primarily performed in forums. When they are used as occasions for deliberation and education, implementation team meetings, task force meetings, focus groups, town hall meetings, newsletters and Internet notices, conference calls, e-mail and social networking exchanges, podcasts, and strategic plans and implementation documents are all examples of forums. These forums can be used in developing a shared understanding about what needs doing, how, and why.

2. *Seize opportunities to be interpreters and direction givers in areas of uncertainty and difficulty.* Help inspire and mobilize others to figure out what might be done to implement strategies and improve the organization's performance in the eyes of key stakeholders. Helping to turn dangers, threats, and perhaps even crises into manageable implementation challenges is an important visionary leadership task, one that will also promote optimism and resilience and thereby free up people's thinking, energy, and other resources to confront the challenges successfully.

3. *Offer compelling visions of the future.* Leaders convey shared visions through stories rooted in shared history yet focused on the future. Effective stories are rich with metaphors that make sense of people's experience, are comprehensive yet open-ended, and impel people toward common ground and shared accomplishment (Terry, 2001). Leaders transmit their own belief in their visionary stories through vivid, energetic, optimistic language (Kouzes & Posner, 2008; Shamir, Arthur, & House, 1994).

4. *Champion new and improved ideas for addressing strategy and implementation challenges.* Championing ideas for addressing implementation challenges is not the same as championing the process of implementation but is nonetheless important. Astute leaders foster an atmosphere in which learning, improvements, and innovative approaches can flourish. These leaders champion ideas that have emerged from practice and been refined by critical reflection, including ethical analysis. In analyzing ideas, leaders keep implementers focused on the important outcomes they seek (Nutt, 2002).

5. *Articulate desired actions and expected consequences.* Pragmatic visionary leaders ensure that actions and consequences are an integral part of and flow from organizational, collaboration, or community visions, missions, and strategies. These will naturally become more detailed as implementation proceeds

(Mintzberg & Westley, 1992) and, in addition to desired actions, should include things the organization, collaboration, or community will stop doing.

Making and Executing Decisions in Arenas

Political leadership is also required of public and nonprofit leaders, in part because all organizations have their political aspects but, more important, because public and nonprofit organizations are inherently involved in politicized decision making much of the time (Bolman & Deal, 2008). Effective political leadership depends on understanding how intergroup power relationships shape decision making and implementation outcomes. Particularly important is understanding how to affect outcomes by having some things never come up for a decision. Specifically, political leaders must undertake the following responsibilities:

1. *Understand the design and use of arenas.* Politically astute leaders must be skilled in designing and using the formal and informal arenas in which decisions are made concerning the implementation of policies, programs, projects, strategies, and other aspects of strategic plans (Crosby & Bryson, 2005). For governmental organizations, these arenas or decision-making venues may be legislative, executive, or administrative—for example, a city council, a mayor's or city manager's office, or a department head's office, respectively. For nonprofit organizations, internal arenas will include board and management meetings, which will also be affected by a variety of governmental arenas. Collaborations and communities will be dependent on many relevant arenas. It is in arenas that the products of forums (such as refined strategy statements, implementation team action plans, or project proposals) are adopted as is, altered, or rejected. A major issue in any implementation process is how to sequence the move from dialogue in forums, particularly implementation team meetings, to decision-making arenas. A large fraction of the necessary strategic and operational thinking will occur as part of the dialogue and discussion in forums. Once viable proposals have been worked out, they then can be moved to arenas for any necessary revisions, adoption, and implementation—or else rejection. At a minimum, managing the transition from forums to arenas depends on figuring out when key decision points will occur and then designing the implementation process to fit those points in such a way that decisions in arenas can be influenced constructively by the work done in forums. A further issue is how to handle any residual conflicts or disputes that may arise during implementation (see below). Some advance thinking is therefore almost always in order about how these residual or subsidiary conflicts might be handled constructively.

2. *Mediate and shape conflict within and among stakeholders.* Conflict is to be expected as part of any significant implementation effort. Political leaders must

have conflict management skills for dealing with followers, other leaders, and various key stakeholders who are in disagreement or have conflicting agendas. To forge winning coalitions, leaders must also bargain and negotiate, inventing options for mutual gain so that they can trade things of value that they control for others' support (Thompson, 2008).

3. *Understand the dynamics of political influence and how to target resources appropriately.* Knowing whom to influence is a requirement for affecting political decision making. Knowing who controls the agenda of the relevant decision-making body, which may be a city council, a board of directors, or some other group, is important knowledge. The next requirement is knowing how to influence. What forms of providing information, lobbying, vote trading, arm-twisting, and so on are acceptable? Another possibility may be trying to change the composition of the decision-making bodies. Basically, political leaders manipulate the costs and benefits of actions so supporters are more motivated to act in desired directions and opponents are less motivated to resist.

Leaders can affect outcomes in arenas dramatically by *influencing the agenda* of what comes up for decision and what does not, thereby becoming a *nondecision* (Bachrach & Baratz, 1963; Crosby & Bryson, 2005). Leaders also can affect outcomes by *strategic voting*, in which participants use their knowledge of voting rules and manipulation of their vote resource to steer outcomes in directions they favor. A final way of influencing outcomes is by *issue framing*—or shaping the way issues are viewed—which can dramatically affect how people vote (Riker, 1986).

4. *Build winning, sustainable coalitions.* Implementation success depends on having a coalition of support for the process and the desired outcomes (Bolman & Deal, 2008). The coalition in place must be strong enough to protect and support strategies during implementation. Building winning coalitions can be pretty gritty work. As Riker (1986, p. 52) notes, "Politics is winning and losing, which depend, mostly, on how large and strong one side is relative to the other. The actions of politics consist in making agreements to join people in alliances and coalitions—hardly the stuff to release readers' adrenaline as do seductions, quarrels, or chases." Ideally, implementers will support the mission, vision, goals, and strategies in the strategic plan; if not, persuasion and education may be necessary, and so too may be making deals in which something is traded in exchange for that support.

5. *Avoid bureaucratic imprisonment.* Political leaders in government, particularly, may find their ability to make and implement needed decisions severely constrained by the bureaucracies in which they serve. Those bureaucracies usually have intricate institutionalized rules and procedures and entrenched personnel that hamper any kind of change. Leaders committed to change must

continuously challenge the rules or else find a way around them. Whenever possible, they should try to win over members of the bureaucracy—for example, by appealing to shared goals (Behn, 1999)—or by enlisting insiders distressed by the inhibiting aspects of rules (Kelman, 2005). When necessary, they should appeal over the heads of resistant bureaucrats to high-level decision makers or to key external stakeholders (Hill & Lynn, 2008; Kouzes & Posner, 2008).

Enforcing Norms, Settling Disputes, and Managing Residual Conflicts

Leaders are always called upon to be ethical, including when they are handling conflict. Disputes and residual conflicts are likely to arise during the implementation of strategies. The decisions made in arenas are unlikely to cover all of the details and difficulties that may come up during implementation. These residual or subsidiary conflicts must be handled constructively, either in other arenas or through the use of formal or informal courts, both to address the difficulty at hand *and* to reinforce or change important norms governing the organization. The following tasks are vital to exercising ethical leadership:

1. *Understand the design and use of formal and informal courts.* Courts operate whenever two actors having a conflict rely on a third party (leader, manager, facilitator, mediator, arbitrator, judge) to help them address it. Managing conflict and settling disputes not only takes care of the issue at hand but also reinforces the important societal or organizational norms used to handle conflict. Leaders must be skilled in the design and use of formal and informal courts, the characteristic settings for enforcing ethical principles, constitutions, and laws and for managing residual conflicts and settling disputes (Crosby & Bryson, 2005). Theoretically, formal courts provide the ultimate social sanctions for conduct mandated or promoted through formal policymaking arenas, but in practice the informal court of public opinion can be even more powerful.

2. *Foster organizational (or collaboration or community) integrity and educate others about ethics, constitutions, laws, and norms.* In nurturing public and nonprofit organizations, collaborations, and communities that advance the common good, leaders must adopt practices and systems that align collective actions with espoused principles (Frederickson, 1997). Such leaders make a public commitment to ethical principles and then manifest them in their own behavior. They involve stakeholders in ethical analysis and decision making, inculcate a sense of personal responsibility in followers, and reward ethical behavior.

3. *Apply constitutions, laws, and norms to specific cases.* Constitutions are usually broad frameworks establishing basic organizational purposes, structures,

and procedures. Laws, while much more narrowly drawn, still typically apply to broad classes of people or actions; moreover, they may emerge from the legislative process containing purposeful omissions and generalities that were necessary to obtain enough votes for passage (Posner, 1985). Therefore, both constitutions and laws require authoritative interpretation as they are applied to specific cases. Outside the formal courts, leaders typically must apply norms rather than laws.

4. *Adapt constitutions, laws, and norms to changing times.* Judicial principles endure even as the conditions that prompted them and the people who created them change dramatically. Sometimes public leaders are able to reshape the law to current needs in legislative, executive, or administrative arenas; often, however, as Neely (1981) suggests, leaders must ask formal courts to mandate a change because vested interests that tend to oppose change hold sway over the executive and legislative branches. In other words, sometimes strategic issues involve the need to change the rules for making rules (Hill & Hupe, 2009).

5. *Resolve conflicts among constitutions, laws, and norms.* Ethical leaders working through the courts must find legitimate bases for deciding among conflicting principles. This may mean relying on judicial enforcement or on a reconciliation of constitutions, laws, and norms. Conflict management and dispute resolution methods typically emphasize the desirability of finding principles or norms that all can support as legitimate bases for settling disputes (Fisher & Ury, 1991; Thompson, 2008).

Obviously, these principles and norms should be applied in such a way that the public interest is served and the common good advanced.

Summary: Putting It All Together and Preparing for Ongoing Strategic Change

The tasks of implementation leadership are complex and many. No single person or group can perform them all (except perhaps for small projects or in small organizations). Effective implementation is a collective phenomenon, typically involving sponsors (which may be policy boards), champions, facilitators, implementation teams, task forces, and others in various ways at various times. Over the course of an implementation cycle, leaders of many different kinds must put together the elements we have described in such a way that organizational, collaboration, or community effectiveness is enhanced via meeting the entity's mandates, fulfilling its mission, achieving its goals, and creating public value. Reflection and deliberation are typically required at many points along the way to consider whether the right people are in the right roles at the right time; whether the content and pace of implementation and the approach to it should be modified; what has been accomplished so far; and what remains to be done. By maintaining awareness of progress, celebrating resilience in the face of setbacks, publicizing the tangible and intangible benefits of the planning process, and continuously developing collective leadership and followership, leaders can help their organizations, collaborations, and communities to satisfy their key stakeholders and advance the common good—and also prepare for the next round of strategic planning.

Worksheet Directions

1. A number of worksheets in Bryson and Alston's *Creating Your Strategic Plan* (2011) can help with assessing leadership in context. The worksheets in Step 4, especially, can assist you in assessing the environment to identify strengths, weaknesses, opportunities, and challenges (or threats).

2. Successful implementation efforts typically have very effective sponsors— persons with enough power and authority to legitimize and support the effort and keep things on track. Use Worksheet 4 to identify and evaluate potential sponsors.

3. Successful implementation also depends on having one or more effective process champions, meaning individuals who will be there on a day-to-day basis to keep things moving. Use Worksheet 5 to identify and evaluate potential champions.

4. Often organizations will establish an implementation coordinating committee (ICC) to make sure that all the varied implementation efforts are aligned and mutually supported and to address important conflicts that arise. Use Worksheet 6 to identify and assess potential members of the ICC.

5. Worksheet 7 can assist your organization in developing a charge or charter for its ICC and related subgroups.

6. Much implementation work takes place in forums for developing and discussing the process. The conversation in forums is often very creative and freewheeling as ideas are developed and evaluated. Decisions are not made in forums but in decision-making arenas, where the dynamic is often very different. In arenas deliberations are typically focused on specific recommendations for action, and the atmosphere is much more formal than it is in forums. Thus, when the time comes for the work of forums to be translated into action, arenas may need to be involved—for example, if a formal decision from a policymaking body is required to proceed. Formal or informal courts may also need to be involved when two actors are having a conflict that a third party must help

to resolve. Often careful planning is needed to make sure the work of forums gets to the appropriate arenas or courts for consideration. Use Worksheet 8 for guidance in developing useful linkages among forums, arenas, and courts.

7. A final tool that may be of use at this point to those faced with leading an implementation effort is Worksheet 9, on values to sustain innovation and change. This worksheet derives from Paul Light's (1998) work on values that seem to characterize organizations that succeed at sustained innovation and change. However, leaders might also decide to postpone using this worksheet until Step 5, when the organization's mandates, mission, vision, and values are examined.

WORKSHEET 4

Implementation Process Sponsors

Instructions. Implementation sponsors are necessary for successful implementation because they have enough prestige, power, and authority to commit the organization to implementing strategies and the strategic plan and to hold people accountable for carrying out implementation efforts.

Implementation sponsors should be able to do the following (or should have the following job description):

1. Articulate the purpose and importance of the implementation effort.

2. Commit necessary resources—time, money, energy, legitimacy—to the effort.

3. Emphasize throughout the implementation process that results will be and are being produced that are important to the organization's mission, mandates, and key stakeholders and that public value will be and is being created.

4. Encourage and reward hard work, smart and creative thinking, constructive dialogue, and multiple sources of input and insight aimed at ensuring successful implementation.

5. Be aware of the possible need for outside consultants.

6. Be willing to exercise power and authority to keep the process on track.

In the following checklists, check the positions existing and potential sponsors hold, and then in the following workspace, list who the implementation sponsors are or need to be, assess their strengths as sponsors, and note any areas where they may need some help.

---

1. Existing sponsors are (check as many as apply):
    ☐ Policy board
    ☐ Chief executive or executive director
    ☐ Line manager
    ☐ Frontline staff
    ☐ External stakeholder
    ☐ Other

2. Potentially needed additional sponsors are (check as many as apply):
    ☐ Policy board
    ☐ Chief executive or executive director
    ☐ Line manager
    ☐ Frontline staff
    ☐ External stakeholder
    ☐ Other

3. Who are the existing and potential sponsors?

Existing or Needed (note which) Implementation Process Sponsors	Strengths They Bring to the Implementation Effort	Areas Where They Will Need Some Help

4. Do we have or can we have a sponsor who can (or sponsors who collectively can) effectively perform the six tasks outlined at the beginning of this worksheet?

☐ Yes

☐ No

☐ Maybe

5. If the response to question 4 is no or maybe, what can be done to ensure effective implementation sponsorship?

Worksheet 4

WORKSHEET 5

Implementation Process Champions

Instructions. Implementation process champions are the people who have primary responsibility for managing implementation efforts on a day-to-day basis.

Champions should be able to do the following (or have the following job description):

1. Keep strategy and strategic plan implementation high on people's agendas.

2. Think about what has to come together (people, information, resources, completed work) at or before key decision points.

3. Keep rallying participants and pushing the implementation process along.

4. Develop champions throughout the organization.

5. Be sensitive to power differences and able to engage all implementers and find ways to share power in order to increase the chances of implementation success.

In the following checklists, check the positions existing and potential implementation champions hold, and then in the following workspace, list who the champions are or need to be, assess their strengths as champions, and note any areas where they may need some help.

1. Existing champions are (check as many as apply):

☐ Policy board member
☐ Chief executive or executive director
☐ Line manager
☐ Frontline staff member
☐ External stakeholder
☐ Volunteer
☐ Other

2. Potentially needed additional champions are (check as many as apply):

☐ Policy board member
☐ Chief executive or executive director
☐ Line manager
☐ Frontline staff member
☐ External stakeholder
☐ Volunteer
☐ Other

3. Who are the existing and potential champions?

Existing or Needed (note which) Implementation Process Champions	Strengths They Bring to the Implementation Effort	Areas Where They Will Need Some Help

4. Do we have or can we have a champion who can (or champions who collectively can) effectively perform the tasks outlined at the beginning of this worksheet?

☐ Yes

☐ No

☐ Maybe

5. If the answer to question 4 is no or maybe, what can be done to ensure effective implementation champions are in place?

Worksheet 5

Implementing and Sustaining Your Strategic Plan.

WORKSHEET 6

Identifying Possible Members of the Implementation Coordinating Committee

Instructions. An implementation coordinating committee (ICC) can help facilitate, connect, and coordinate structures, processes, resources, or activities across organizational boundaries in ways required for successful implementation. ICC members—particularly when they are sponsors and champions—can bring together the information, political support, authority, and personnel necessary to move ahead in reasonable and timely ways. The ICC can provide a central focal point for implementation-related dialogue and integration. The ICC is also a venue where difficulties can be worked out in reasonable, amicable ways away of the limelight.

ICCs should be able to do the following (and perhaps have these responsibilities included in a formal charter):

1. Focus collective attention across boundaries on strategy and strategic plan implementation tasks, responsibilities, progress, and needed further action.

2. Help with coordinating the implementation process and tasks across boundaries of various sorts.

3. Rally key participants, and push the implementation process along.

4. Provide a venue in which power may be shared.

5. Offer a setting where important conflicts may be explored and managed effectively.

6. Provide occasions for the development of implementation champions throughout the organization.

In the following checklists, check the kinds of people already on the ICC and potentially needed new members of the ICC, and then in the following workspace, assess their strengths as ICC members, and note any areas where they may need some help.

1. Existing ICC members are (check as many as apply):

   ☐ Policy board member
   ☐ Chief executive or executive director
   ☐ Line manager
   ☐ Frontline staff member
   ☐ External stakeholder
   ☐ Budgeting or financial management specialist
   ☐ Human resource specialist
   ☐ Information technology specialist
   ☐ Volunteer
   ☐ Outside stakeholder
   ☐ Other

2. Potentially needed additional ICC members are (check as many as apply):

   ☐ Policy board member
   ☐ Chief executive or executive director
   ☐ Line manager
   ☐ Frontline staff member
   ☐ External stakeholder
   ☐ Budgeting or financial management specialist
   ☐ Human resource specialist
   ☐ Information technology specialist
   ☐ Outside stakeholder
   ☐ Volunteer
   ☐ Other

3. Who are the existing and potential committee members?

Existing or Needed (note which) Implementation Coordinating Committee Members	Strengths They Bring to the Implementation Effort	Areas Where They Will Need Some Help

4. Do we have or can we have an ICC that can effectively perform the tasks outlined at the beginning of this worksheet?

☐ Yes

☐ No

☐ Maybe

5. If the answer to question 4 is no or maybe, what can be done to ensure an effective ICC is in place?

Worksheet 6

Implementing and Sustaining Your Strategic Plan.

WORKSHEET 7

Developing a Charge for the Implementation Coordinating Committee and Related Subgroups

Instructions. Complete this worksheet as part of the process of developing a charge or charter for your organization's ICC and related subgroups (referred to here as Team A, Team B, and Team C).

Implementation Coordinating Committee

Members	Committee Roles and Responsibilities	Starting and Ending Dates of Assignment	Committee Reporting Relationships for Implementation

Strategic Goal #1	Charge/Task	Membership	Each Member's Knowledge Base and Competencies	Roles and Responsibilities	Starting and Ending Dates	Reporting Relationships for the Task
Team A						
Team B						
Team C						

Strategic Goal #2	Charge/Task	Membership	Each Member's Knowledge Base and Competencies	Roles and Responsibilities	Starting and Ending Dates	Reporting Relationships for the Task
Team A						
Team B						
Team C						

Worksheet 7

Implementing and Sustaining Your Strategic Plan. Copyright © 2011 by John Wiley & Sons, Inc. All rights reserved.

Strategic Goal #3	Charge/Task	Membership	Each Member's Knowledge Base and Competencies	Roles and Responsibilities	Starting and Ending Dates	Reporting Relationships for the Task
Team A						
Team B						
Team C						

Worksheet 7

Implementing and Sustaining Your Strategic Plan. Copyright © 2011 by John Wiley & Sons, Inc. All rights reserved.

WORKSHEET 8

Understanding and Linking Forums, Arenas, and Courts

Instructions. Formal and informal forums, arenas, and courts are the places where, respectively, dialogue and discussion occur, decisions are made, and residual disputes are managed and the underlying norms in the system are reinforced or changed. Typical *forums* for dialogue, deliberation, and education are implementation team meetings, task force meetings, focus groups, town hall meetings, newsletters and Internet notices, conference calls, e-mail and social networking exchanges, podcasts, and strategic plans and implementation documents. Both formal and informal forums are typically far more flexible in design and use than are formal arenas and courts.

Typical *arenas* for making decisions concerning the implementation of policies, programs, projects, strategies, and other aspects of strategic plans may vary with organizational type. For governmental organizations, arenas include legislative, executive, or administrative venues, such as, respectively, a city council, a mayor's or city manager's office, or a department head's office. For nonprofit organizations, internal arenas include the board and management meetings, which will also be affected by a variety of governmental arenas. Collaborations and communities will be dependent on many relevant arenas. It is in arenas that the products of forums (such as refined strategy statements, implementation team action plans, or project proposals) are adopted as is, altered, or rejected. A major issue in any implementation process is how to sequence the move from dialogue in forums, particularly implementation team meetings, to decision making in arenas.

Formal and informal *courts* operate whenever two actors having a conflict rely on a third party (leader, manager, facilitator, mediator, arbitrator, judge, public opinion) to help them address it. Managing conflict and settling disputes not only takes care of the issue at hand but also reinforces the important societal or organizational norms used to handle conflict. Theoretically, formal courts provide the ultimate social sanctions for conduct mandated or promoted through formal policymaking arenas, but in practice the informal court of public opinion can be even more powerful.

A large fraction of the necessary strategic and operational implementation-related thinking will occur as part of the dialogue and discussion in forums. Once viable proposals have been worked out, they then can be moved to arenas for any necessary revisions, adoption, and implementation—or else rejection. At a minimum, managing the transition from forums to arenas depends on figuring out when key decision points will occur and then designing the implementation process to fit those points in such a way that decisions in arenas can be influenced constructively by the work done in forums. A further issue is how to handle any residual conflicts or disputes that may arise during implementation. Some advance thinking is therefore almost always in order about how these residual or subsidiary conflicts might be handled constructively in informal or formal courts.

In the worksheet that follows, consider the suitability for implementation purposes of the design and typical use of your organization's existing forums, arenas, and courts and possible changes that might be needed in them. Then consider whether implementation purposes might be better served by creating new (or additional) forums, arenas, and courts. Reconsider the responses on this worksheet after completing the worksheets in Part 4 (Steps 7 through 11), concerning resourcing and structuring implementation, alignment, and ongoing learning. Note that successful pursuit of different aspects of strategy implementation and the strategic plan are likely to rely on different sets of forums, arenas, and courts. So fill out as many worksheets as are necessary to cover all important aspects of the implementation process.

1. Implementation aspect being considered:

2. Forums help people think about matters of concern through dialogue and deliberation. In which forums will implementation-related dialogue and deliberation occur? List the relevant existing formal and informal forums for this aspect of the implementation process and any changes to them that might be needed.

Existing Formal and Informal Forums	Characteristics and Membership	Needed Changes

Worksheet 8

Implementing and Sustaining Your Strategic Plan.

Comments:

Needed New Forums	Characteristics and Membership	What the Forum Adds to the Mix

Comments:

Worksheet 8

Implementing and Sustaining Your Strategic Plan.

3. Arenas (legislative, executive, or administrative) are where implementation-related decisions are made. List the relevant existing formal and informal arenas for this aspect of the implementation process, and any changes to them that might be needed.

Existing Formal and Informal Arenas	Characteristics and Membership	Needed Changes

Comments:

Needed New Arenas	Characteristics and Membership	What the Arena Adds to the Mix

Worksheet 8

Implementing and Sustaining Your Strategic Plan.

Comments:

4. Formal and informal courts (formal courts or tribunals, administrative law courts, the court of public opinion, and so on) are where residual disputes (those not settled by arenas) are addressed and resolved. List the relevant existing formal and informal courts for this aspect of the implementation process, and any changes to them that might be needed.

Existing Formal and Informal Courts	Characteristics and Membership	Needed Changes

Comments:

Worksheet 8

Implementing and Sustaining Your Strategic Plan.

Needed New Courts	Characteristics and Membership	What the Court Adds to the Mix

Comments:

Worksheet 8

Implementing and Sustaining Your Strategic Plan.

WORKSHEET 9

Values to Sustain Innovation and Change

Instructions. Paul Light's important work indicates that successful innovation and change has a foundation in four core values of organizational life (Paul C. Light, *Sustaining Innovation: Creating Nonprofit and Government Organizations that Innovate Naturally* [San Francisco: Jossey-Bass/ Wiley, 1998], pp. 245–253). These values provide a crucial context for effective assessment, learning, and action in pursuit of organizational goals. The four values are

Honesty

- Willingness to tell the truth (no surprises)
- Clearly communicating about reality
- Inviting risk and tolerating mistakes

Trust

- Believing in the people
- Pushing authority downward (democratizing)
- Calling for new ideas
- Listening and learning (not repeating mistakes)
- Lowering barriers to internal collaboration

Rigor

- Measuring results
- Celebrating success
- Hard-nosed forecasting
- Working hard and strategically building mission into systems

Faith

- Moving or leaping beyond known experience
- Believing in self in the winds of change

1. Have individual members of the leadership group rate the organization on the following core values of innovating organizations:

	Good	Average	Poor	**Future Priority and Notes to Improve**
Honesty				
Trust				
Rigor/hard work				
Faith/hope				

2. After the results have been compiled, have the leadership group (implementation coordinating committee, sponsors, champions, and others) discuss the results and what they might mean for achieving success in implementation success.

Worksheet 9

Implementing and Sustaining Your Strategic Plan.

Understanding How and Why the Strategic Plan Came to Be

Purpose of Step

The purpose of Step 3 is to help implementers beyond sponsors, champions, and the implementation coordinating committee (ICC) understand more about the implementation context by identifying and clarifying any lessons to be drawn from the organization's experience with previous change efforts, and by examining the origins of the strategic plan and adopted strategies. As Antonio says in William Shakespeare's *The Tempest*, "what's past is prologue" (II, i, 253). Implementers will want to carry forward what has worked well in the past and figure out what to do about what has not worked well.

Implementation should be viewed as an integral part of an organization's ongoing history. Implementation takes part within a web of prior understandings, relationships, strategies, job holders and job descriptions, competencies, routines, practices, prior resource allocations, and so on. If the implementers are different from the strategic planners, it can be very helpful—and prudent—to learn the circumstances out of which the new strategic plan grew, because the upcoming implementation effort's future will in part be a carrying forward of what has preceded that effort. As William Faulkner observed in *Requiem for a Nun* (1951), "The past is never dead. It's not even past."

Possible Desired Implementation Outcomes

- Clarity about the history of the strategic plan, including

  a. The reasons for creating a strategic plan

  b. The process that was followed, and how well it worked or did not work

  c. The people and groups involved in plan preparation, and the ways they were involved

d. The issues addressed as part of the strategic planning process

e. The commitments made as part of reaching agreement on the final plan regarding

Leadership

Resources

Reporting on progress, difficulties, and results

Ongoing problem solving

Stakeholder engagement

f. The manner in which the final decision was made to adopt and proceed

g. The issues left unresolved

- Collection of all relevant background materials from the strategic planning process, including those related to

a. Clarification of mission, vision, and values

b. Organizational mandates

c. Stakeholder analyses

d. SWOC/T analyses

e. Assessment of competencies

f. Existing and proposed strategies

g. Status and effectiveness of performance management systems

- Reflection on the lessons to be learned from the organization's previous experience with change efforts, going back at least several years and perhaps five to ten years

Worksheet and Exercise Directions

1. Someone should assemble in one place (physically or on a Web site) the most recent version of the strategic plan and all the relevant background materials.

2. Next, implementation planners (perhaps the ICC) should brainstorm a list of people who should be interviewed to assemble the story of the strategic plan's preparation and pull together the implications of the strategic planning process for strategic plan implementation, including any obvious requirements for implementation success. The group to be interviewed will likely be somewhat different from and larger than that involved in any implementation readiness assessment interviews that may have been conducted. Worksheet 1 (Step 1) provides a set of potential interview questions.

3. Implementation planners should reflect as a group on what they have learned via the interview process and prepare a set of apposite guidelines to facilitate the implementation process. Action plans should be developed immediately to respond to what was learned from the interviews, perhaps including capturing any quick wins or low-hanging fruit. See Worksheet 10 for a possible format for a meeting to review interview results.

4. Consider engaging implementers and others in an "organizational highs and lows exercise," if that exercise was not already used by these people during Step 4 of the strategic planning process. Again, implications for the upcoming implementation effort should be drawn from this exercise, including any apparent requirements for implementation success. See Exercise 1 for guidance on engaging in this exercise.

Exercise 1: Lessons About Successful and Unsuccessful Change Management from Reviewing the Organization's Highs and Lows

Often organizational members can learn how to pursue successful changes in their organizations by comparing and contrasting the causes of memorably positive (highs) and negative (lows) organizational events. The further back people look, the better able they are to look forward (Kouzes & Posner, 2008). Implementation efforts may involve both highs and lows, so understanding what characterized the highs as well as the lows can help members achieve more implementation highs and avoid implementation lows. The following exercise is patterned after one for individuals outlined in Crosby and Bryson (2005, p.50), which in turn is based on a more elaborate charting exercise described by Kouzes and Posner (2002). The exercise consists of the following steps:

1. Reserve a room with a large wall. A room with a whiteboard that covers a whole wall is ideal. Alternatively, you might wish to cover a wall with sheets of flipchart paper taped together (two rows of eight sheets each), so that the results of the exercise can be saved intact.

2. Divide the wall into top and bottom halves by drawing a horizontal line on the whiteboard or flipchart sheets with a marker or by applying a long strip of masking tape.

3. At the right-hand end of the line, write in the current year. At the left-hand end, write in the date that is as far back in time as you wish the implementation planning team to ultimately look forward in time (typically the duration of the current strategic plan or longer).

4. Ask group members to individually and silently brainstorm, on a sheet of scratch paper, all of the organizational highs and lows they can recall that occurred within the agreed time frame. These events might include the organization's founding, arrivals or departures of key leaders, successful or unsuccessful management of crises, particularly useful or disastrous innovations, prior strategic planning efforts, and so on. Participants should date each item and label it as a high or low.

5. Have participants transcribe their highs and lows onto half sheets of paper, one high or low per sheet (or else write them on large Post-it® notes). Once this is done, a piece of tape rolled sticky side out or a small bit of self-adhesive putty is attached to the back of each sheet.

6. Have participants stick their sheets to the wall at the appropriate place on the timeline. The height

(continued)

(continued)

of each sheet above or below the line should reflect just how high the high was or how low the low was.

7. Ask the group to identify the themes that were common to the highs, to the lows, and to both. What patterns emerge across the highs and across the lows? Are the highs and lows related to one another in any way? Probe some around the role of emotion in relation to the highs and lows. Someone should be the designated note taker for this and subsequent steps.

8. Then ask the group to further analyze the data and themes by answering these questions:

   - What is common to the highs (or subsets of highs)? What made them highs? What did we do or not do, and what was out of our control?

   - What is common to the lows (or subsets of lows)? What made them lows? What did we do or not do, and what was out of our control?

   - What lessons can we draw for successfully managing strategy implementation and change?

   - What seems to be absolutely necessary for us if we are to manage challenges successfully?

   - What helps us manage challenges successfully, but does not seem to be absolutely necessary?

9. Identify what the organization's strategies have been in practice—what has actually happened, as opposed to what might be voiced in official pronouncements. Ask what the organization seems to be particularly good at doing; probe for ambitions and competencies and how they have been linked. Also ask what the organization does not do well; look for problems with aspirations, competencies, or both.

10. To conclude the discussion, have the group move the timeline forward an equivalent distance and discuss what group members' previous analyses might imply for the future and especially for implementation of the strategic plan. What themes, patterns, and strategies from the past would the group like to see projected into the future? Which would the group not like to see projected? What new themes would the group like to see?

Agenda for Follow-Up Meeting to Assess Results of Interviews of Strategic Plan Preparers and Adopters

Instructions. The interviews conducted at the outset of the implementation process (see Worksheet 1), and any done subsequently, provide the source materials for an important learning occasion for implementation planners, in which they draw the implications for implementation from the interviewees' responses. Prior to the meeting at which this learning takes place, someone or a small group should prepare a question-by-question summary of the interview results. This summary should be circulated in advance.

Depending on the number of interviews and the issues they raise, the meeting might last from ninety minutes to a full day. Depending on the circumstances, professional facilitation may be advisable. After the purpose of the meeting is stated and participants are introduced, the meeting's agenda should be organized around the following set of questions:

1. What are your overall impressions of the content of the interviews you conducted and the summary of interviewee responses?

2. Go through the summary question by question, taking note of the following:

   a. What are the important strengths of the organization and the strategic planning process?

   b. What areas are in need of attention?

   c. What suggestions do interviewees have for specific improvements?

3. What do interviewees say is absolutely necessary for implementation success? Why do they think it is necessary?

4. What additional things—features, factors, resources, and the like—would contribute to implementation success but are not absolutely necessary? Why or how do interviewees think these things would help?

5. Based on the discussion, have any overall impressions changed?

Worksheet 10

Implementing and Sustaining Your Strategic Plan.

6. What is our action plan for follow-up?

Action	Person Responsible	Due Date

Clarifying Who the Implementation Stakeholders Are

Purpose of Step

The purpose of Step 4 is to clarify who the implementation stakeholders are, what matters to them, and whether and how they might affect or be involved in implementation efforts. The key to success for public and nonprofit organizations is satisfying important stakeholders according to each stakeholder's criteria for satisfaction. Implementation efforts are likely to fail if they do not satisfy key stakeholders.

Stakeholders

A stakeholder is any person, group, or organization that can place a claim on the organization's resources, attention, or output or is affected by its output. A stakeholder analysis is the means for identifying who the organization's internal and external stakeholders are, how they evaluate the organization, how they influence the organization and its implementation efforts, what the organization needs from them, and how important they are. A stakeholder analysis is particularly useful in providing valuable information about the political situation facing the organization.

A stakeholder analysis should have occurred as part of the organization's strategic planning process. The results of that analysis should have informed the development and refinement of a mission statement (and perhaps vision and values statements as well) and helped the organization determine who should be involved in the strategic planning process and in what ways. That analysis may be updated to inform implementation efforts. (Steps 1, 2, and 3 in this workbook may have involved implementation teams in some preliminary stakeholder analysis.) Whom you involve in implementation and how you involve them will go a long way toward determining in practice who claims ownership of the process and how successful the organization is likely to be in implementing its new strategies and strategic plans. Additional detailed advice on stakeholder analyses can be found in *Strategic Planning for Public and Nonprofit Organizations*, fourth edition (Bryson, 2011, especially Chapters Three and Four and Resource A; also see Bryson, 2004).

Possible Desired Implementation Outcomes

- An inclusive list of implementation stakeholders
- A draft analysis of how, where, when, and why to involve these stakeholders in the implementation process (beyond that which was done in Steps 1, 2, and 3)

Worksheet Directions

1. Have the implementation planners (again perhaps the implementation coordinating committee) brainstorm a list of internal and external stakeholders (Worksheet 11) and fill out an analysis worksheet for each stakeholder (Worksheets 12 and 13).

2. Then figure out where each stakeholder should be located on a power versus interest grid (Worksheet 14). The grid arrays stakeholders in terms of their power to affect the organization and their interest in the organization's work and mission. Power versus interest grids typically help implementers to determine which players' interests and power bases *must* be taken into account in order to produce a credible evaluation. More broadly, they also highlight coalitions to be encouraged or discouraged, behavior that should be fostered, and stakeholders whose buy-in should be sought or who should be co-opted, in part by revealing which stakeholders have the most to gain (or lose) and which have the most (or least) control over the implementation process. This information establishes a basis for assessing political, technical, practical, and other risks as implementation goes forward.

   Finally, these grids may provide some information on how to convince stakeholders to change their views. Interestingly, the knowledge gained from a completed power versus interest grid can be used to advance the interests of the relatively powerless subjects (Bryson, Cunningham, & Lokkesmoe, 2002).

3. Next try to understand the extent to which each stakeholder supports or opposes implementation efforts (Worksheet 15). Use this information to determine whether you have the coalition of support you need to effectively pursue and protect implementation efforts, and what might be done to strengthen the coalition and weaken opposition.

4. Figure out who is or should be in the coalition needed to support and protect implementation efforts so that mandates are met, the mission is accomplished, goals are achieved, and significant and lasting public value is created (use Worksheet 16).

5. Finally, on the basis of these analyses, determine how best to engage stakeholders in the implementation process (Worksheets 17 and 18). If planned strategies and other aspects of the strategic plan are to be implemented, both the implementation process and the results need to involve or speak to key stakeholders in significant ways. Engaging stakeholders appropriately is hard work, and you probably cannot please everyone. Nonetheless, it is worth trying to satisfy key stakeholders to the extent possible—as long as all important features of adopted strategies are maintained.

WORKSHEET 11

Implementation Stakeholder Identification

Instructions. The starting place for conducting an implementation stakeholder analysis is to list the organization's stakeholders. Be as inclusive as possible the first time around in filling out the worksheet that follows. Later you and your group might consider deciding what importance each stakeholder has in terms of his or her positive or negative impact on implementation and the organization's ability to fulfill its mission, meet its mandates, and create public value through implementation. A stakeholder analysis done early in the implementation process can help you decide who should be involved in the process and when, how, and why. Additional stakeholder analyses may be needed later. Some stakeholders, like unions or policy board members, may be both internal and external stakeholders. On the next page you can see a very general example of how Worksheet 11 might be completed for a public agency. When filling out your worksheet, be more specific than the example is about stakeholder identities—in other words, say *which* state agencies and *which* nonprofit organizations are stakeholders.

Example: The figure on this page displays a very general stakeholder mapping exercise for a public agency. Be more specific when you fill out your own map on the next page.

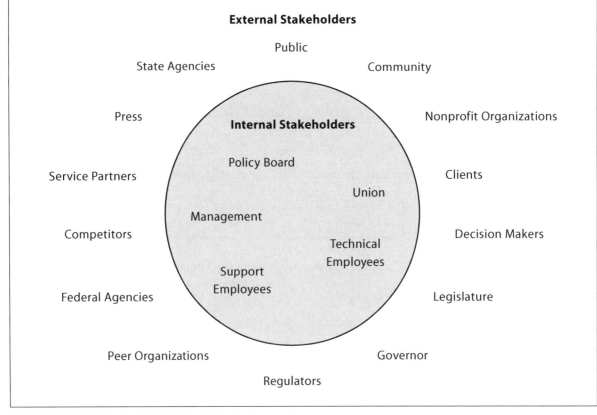

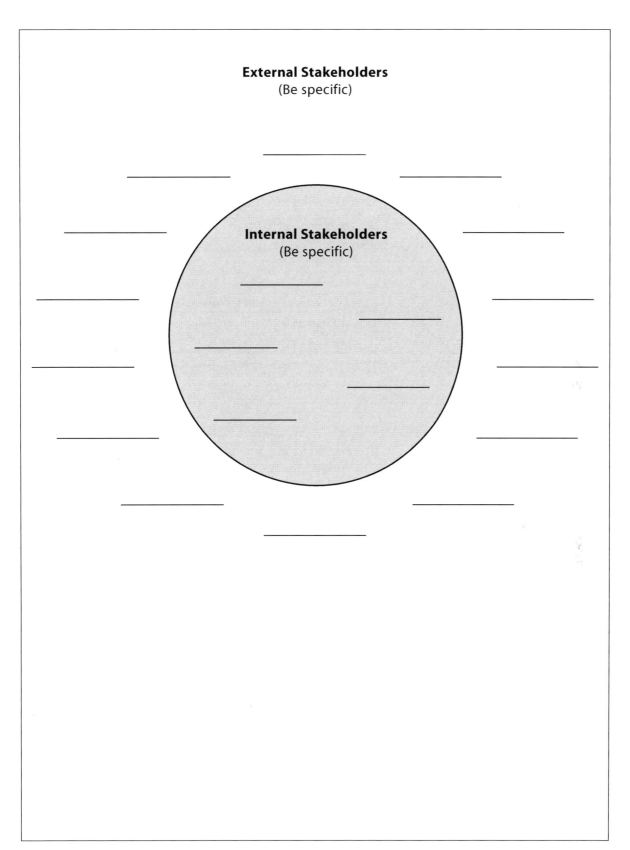

Worksheet 11

Implementing and Sustaining Your Strategic Plan.

WORKSHEET 12

External Implementation Stakeholder Analysis

Instructions. An external implementation stakeholder is any person, group, or organization outside the organization that can make a claim on the organization's attention, resources, or output or is affected by the organization's output. For example, an external implementation stakeholder may be the organization's client or customer for goods and services, a service partner, a funder, a regulatory entity, a union, or taxpayers and the citizenry in general.

For each external implementation stakeholder group listed on Worksheet 11, fill out a separate external implementation stakeholder analysis worksheet. Rank your stakeholders in terms of their importance to your organization's implementation efforts.

Stakeholder's Name:	Type of Stakeholder		
	Client or Customer	Partner	Other

Criteria Used by Stakeholder to Assess Our Performance	Our Sense of Their Judgment About Our Performance		
	Poor	Average	Good

1. How does this stakeholder affect us, and how do we affect this stakeholder?

2. What do we need from this stakeholder, and what does this stakeholder need from us?

3. How important is this stakeholder?

   ☐ Extremely
   ☐ Reasonably
   ☐ Not at all

4. What role should this stakeholder have in the implementation process, if any?

   ☐ Member of implementation coordinating committee
   ☐ Member of implementation team
   ☐ Participant in the process
   ☐ Periodic reviewer of implementation efforts
   ☐ Decision maker
   ☐ Other

Worksheet 12

WORKSHEET 13

Internal Implementation Stakeholder Analysis

Instructions. An internal stakeholder is any person, group, or other entity inside the organization that can make a claim on the organization's attention, resources, or output or is affected by the organization's output. For example, internal implementation stakeholders may be specific board members, managers, or employees, or entire groups or departments.

For each internal implementation stakeholder individual or group listed on Worksheet 11, fill out a separate internal implementation stakeholder analysis worksheet. Rank your stakeholders in terms of their importance to your organization and their role.

Stakeholder's name: _____

Criteria Used by Stakeholder to Assess Our Performance	Our Sense of Their Judgment About Our Performance		
	Poor	Average	Good

1. How does this stakeholder affect us, and how do we affect this stakeholder?

2. What do we need from this stakeholder, and what does this stakeholder need from us?

3. How important is this stakeholder?

    ☐ Extremely
    ☐ Reasonably
    ☐ Not at all

4. What role should this stakeholder have in the implementation process, if any?

    ☐ Member of implementation coordinating committee
    ☐ Member of implementation team
    ☐ Participant in the process
    ☐ Periodic reviewer of implementation efforts
    ☐ Decision maker
    ☐ Other

WORKSHEET 14

Power Versus Interest Grid

Instructions. Power versus interest grids array stakeholders on a two-by-two matrix (often using Post-it® notes on a flipchart sheet). The dimensions are the stakeholder's interest or stake in the implementation process or results (or some aspect of the process or results) and the stakeholder's power to affect the implementation process or result. *Interest* here means interest in a political sense; that is, having a political stake as opposed to simple inquisitiveness. In reality each of the dimensions is a range, from low to high interest and from low to high power, and stakeholders may be anywhere within those ranges. Nonetheless, it is often helpful to think of stakeholders as generally falling into four categories:

- *Players have both an interest and significant power.* They have a high potential to be deeply engaged in implementation.

- *Subjects have an interest but little power.* It may be important to support and enhance subjects' capacity to be involved, especially when they may be affected by implementation, as might be the case with program participants.

- *Context setters have power but little direct interest.* It may be important to increase the interest of context setters in implementation if they are likely to pose barriers to implementation through their disinterest.

- *The crowd consists of stakeholders with little interest or power.* The crowd may need to be informed about the implementation process and its results. Of course, if communication is badly done, controversy may quickly turn an amorphous crowd into a very interested mob.

On the power versus interest grid that follows (or on a similar grid drawn on flipchart paper), place the name of each of the implementation stakeholders identified in Worksheet 11 in the appropriate place on the grid. The scales are not absolute but relative, so that, for example, within the player category there will be some players who are more powerful or have a stronger interest than others.

Once the stakeholders are arrayed appropriately, discuss the resulting pattern or patterns and what they mean for implementation.

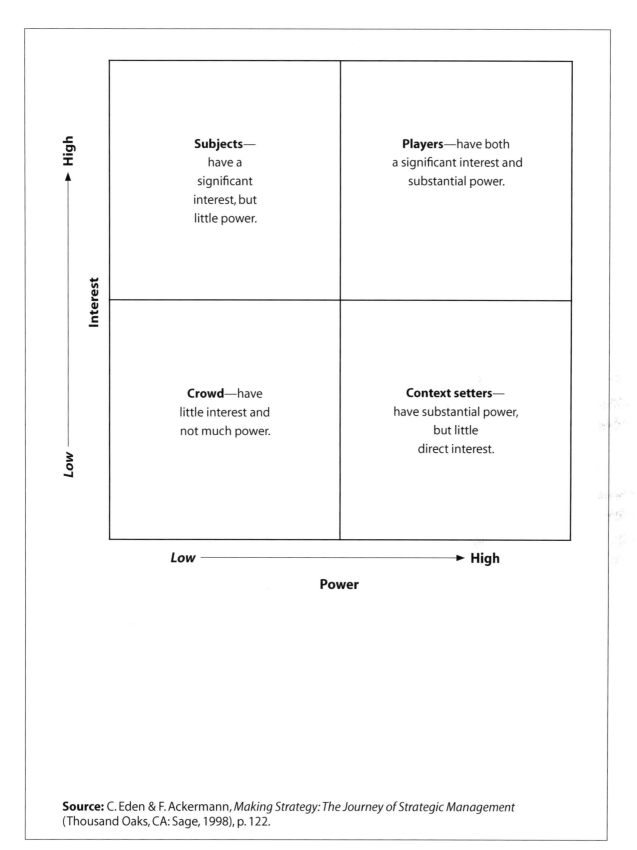

Source: C. Eden & F. Ackermann, *Making Strategy: The Journey of Strategic Management* (Thousand Oaks, CA: Sage, 1998), p. 122.

Worksheet 14

Implementing and Sustaining Your Strategic Plan.

WORKSHEET 15

Implementation Support Versus Opposition

Instructions. Implementation support versus opposition grids indicate which stakeholders are likely to support implementation of strategies and strategic plans (or particular parts of them) and which are likely to oppose them. The steps are simple. On the implementation support versus opposition grid that follows (or on a similar grid drawn on flipchart paper), plot the name of each implementation stakeholder identified in Worksheet 14, placing it where—in the group's judgment—the stakeholder falls in terms of likely support for or opposition to the implementation effort (or aspects of the implementation effort). Discuss and move the names around until the group agrees with the arrangement. Then everyone should step back and reflect on where the implementation effort has the needed support. To the extent that there is stakeholder opposition to what is otherwise seen as desirable, the team may want to assess how the stakeholders in question might be influenced to support, or at least not oppose, the implementation plan. Alternatively, the team might reconsider what is planned to see if stakeholder support can be gained without sacrificing the important merits of the strategy, program, project, or plan.

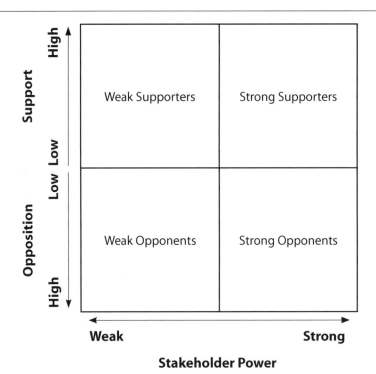

Source: B. C. Crosby, J. M. Bryson, & S. R. Anderson, *Leadership for the Common Good Fieldbook* (St. Paul: University of Minnesota Extension Service, 2003), adapted from P. C. Nutt & R. W. Backoff, *Strategic Management of Public and Third Sector Organizations: A Handbook for Leaders* (San Francisco: Jossey-Bass/Wiley, 1992), p. 198.

WORKSHEET 16

Creating the Supportive Coalition

Instructions. A strong and supportive coalition is a necessary requirement for successful implementation. A coalition can provide needed support and protection for implementation efforts, particularly when there is opposition to those efforts. Coalitions organize around ideas and interests and allow people, groups, and organizations to achieve together what they could not achieve separately. Not every member of a coalition will agree on everything, and that is OK.

Use the following worksheet to figure out who is already in your organization's supportive coalition, and why, and who should be in the coalition but is not, and what might induce them to join. After filling out the worksheet, decide whether you have the necessary coalition of support, and if not, what might be done to create it. If the necessary coalition cannot be created, figure out what might be done about that situation, if anything.

Stakeholders Already in the Coalition	Why the Stakeholder Is in the Coalition

Stakeholders Not Yet in the Coalition Who Should Be	What They Might Want or Need in Order to Join the Coalition

Worksheet 16

WORKSHEET 17

Engaging External Implementation Stakeholders

Instructions. Identifying the organization's stakeholders is an important part of designing and managing a successful implementation process. An organization's stakeholders include any person, group, or organization that can place a claim on the organization's attention, resources, or output, or is affected by that output. Implementation stakeholders are those stakeholders with a particular stake in the implementation process or its results.

Review Worksheets 11, 12, 13, 14, 15, and 16, and then list the key external implementation stakeholders and decide how they should be engaged in the implementation process—or not.

Key External Implementation Stakeholder's Name		Type of Engagement in Implementation				
	Ignore	Inform	Consult	Involve	Collaborate or Partner	Decision-Making Authority
		We will keep you informed of implementation progress and results.	*We will keep you informed, listen to you, and provide feedback on how your input influenced the implementation process.*	*We will work with you to ensure your concerns are considered and reflected in options considered, make sure you get to review and comment on options, and provide feedback on how your input is used in the implementation process.*	*We will incorporate your advice and suggestions to the greatest extent possible, and give you meaningful opportunities to be part of the implementation decision-making process.*	*This is your implementation effort. We will offer options to inform your decisions. You will decide and we will support and facilitate implementing your decisions.*

Name	Ignore	Inform	Consult	Involve	Collaborate/Partner	Decision-Making Authority

Source: Some information on types of involvement adapted from International Association for Public Participation, *Spectrum of Public Participation* (http://www.iap2.org/associations/4748/files/IAP2%20Spectrum_vertical.pdf, 2007).

Worksheet 17

Implementing and Sustaining Your Strategic Plan. Copyright © 2011 by John Wiley & Sons, Inc. All rights reserved.

When you have filled out the table, revisit the question of who needs to be engaged in the implementation process and how. Reconsider membership of external stakeholders on the implementation coordinating committee, implementation team(s), and other relevant bodies. Think about how to engage key external stakeholders in other ways: for example, through focus groups, discussion groups, or surveys.

The ideal size for an implementation team is probably four to seven people, and certainly no more than nine. The team may be a subgroup of a larger group, such as the implementation coordinating committee, although that group also should probably not be too large. There is a trade-off between getting many people involved and still getting some action!

Having said that, we would also advise being as inclusive as possible in engaging stakeholders in other ways. Good suggestions and new ideas will come into the process, and the legitimacy of the process will be enhanced.

Keeping participants informed and appropriately engaged greatly increases ownership of the implementation process and its results. Developing an effective communications plan to keep participants informed of the implementation effort and its progress is typically an important part of an effective implementation process.

Worksheet 17

WORKSHEET 18

Engaging Internal Implementation Stakeholders

Instructions. Identifying the organization's stakeholders is an important part of designing and managing a successful implementation process. An organization's stakeholders include any person, group, or organization that can place a claim on the organization's attention, resources, or output, or is affected by that output. Implementation stakeholders are those stakeholders with a particular stake in the implementation process or its results.

Review Worksheets 11, 12, 13, 14, 15, and 16, and then list the key *internal* implementation stakeholders and decide how they should be engaged in the implementation process—or not.

| Key Internal Implementation Stakeholder's Name | Type of Engagement in Implementation | | | | | |
	Ignore	Inform	Consult	Involve	Collaborate or Partner	Decision-Making Authority
		We will keep you informed of implementation progress and results.	*We will keep you informed, listen to you, and provide feedback on how your input influenced the implementation process.*	*We will work with you to ensure your concerns are considered and reflected in options considered, make sure you get to review and comment on options, and provide feedback on how your input is used in the implementation process.*	*We will incorporate your advice and suggestions to the greatest extent possible, and give you meaningful opportunities to be part of the implementation decision-making process.*	*This is your implementation effort. We will offer options to inform your decisions. You will decide and we will support and facilitate implementing your decisions.*

Source: Some information on types of involvement adapted from International Association for Public Participation, *Spectrum of Public Participation* (http://www.iap2.org/associations/4748/files/IAP2%20Spectrum_vertical.pdf, 2007).

Worksheet 18

Implementing and Sustaining Your Strategic Plan. Copyright © 2011 by John Wiley & Sons, Inc. All rights reserved.

117

When you have filled out the table, revisit the question of who needs to be engaged in the implementation process and how. Reconsider membership of internal stakeholders on the implementation coordinating committee, implementation team(s), and other relevant bodies. Think about how to engage key internal stakeholders in other ways: for example, through focus groups, discussion groups, or surveys.

The ideal size for an implementation team is probably four to seven people, and certainly no more than nine. The team may be a subgroup of a larger group, such as the implementation coordinating committee, although that group also should probably not be too large. There is a trade-off between getting many people involved and still getting some action!

Having said that, we would also advise being as inclusive as possible in engaging stakeholders in other ways. Good suggestions and new ideas will come into the process, and the legitimacy of the process will be enhanced.

Keeping participants informed and appropriately engaged greatly increases ownership of the implementation process and its results. Developing an effective communications plan to keep participants informed of the implementation effort and its progress is typically an important part of an effective implementation process.

Part 3

Clarifying Strategic and Operational Directions

3

Clarifying Direction

Step 5: Articulating what the organization's mandates, mission, vision, and values mean for implementation and alignment

Step 6: Getting clear about strategies that will continue, will be started, or will be phased out

Step 5

Articulating What the Organization's Mandates, Mission, Vision, and Values Mean for Implementation and Alignment

Purpose of Step

The purpose of Step 5 is to help implementers understand more about what the organization's mandates, mission, vision, and values mean for the alignment of high-level purposes with implementation work on the ground. The work of clarifying organizational mandates and developing and refining organizational mission, vision, and values usually occurs during strategic plan preparation. (If this work has not been done, see Steps 2 and 3 in Bryson & Alston's *Creating Your Strategic Plan*, third edition [2011], for assistance with it.) In the current step, the implications of that work for implementation and alignment are explored—in large organizations this exploration is often carried out by persons who were not involved in the strategic planning effort.

Mandates are things the organization is required to do (or not do) and are often imposed by external actors. Mandates may be formal—such as laws, rules, or regulations—or informal—such as political mandates for change or deeply held public expectations. Mandates vary in what they require. Sometimes they require that a particular process or set of activities be followed; at other times they specify that a particular standard or outcomes be achieved.

The *mission* encapsulates the organization's purpose—its reason for existence. A *mission statement* should be action oriented and articulate *what* the organization is here to do, and *why*. The statement should also say, in general, *how* the organization will pursue its work in order to create lasting and significant public value.

Values form an important part of the foundation on which the organization operates. *Value statements* answer these questions: How do we want to conduct our business? How do we want to treat our key stakeholders? What do we really care about—that is, value? Values are part of an organization's culture, so there may very well be a difference between the values people *espouse* and the values actually followed *in practice*.

A *vision statement*—often called a *vision of success*—typically describes what the organization and key parts of its external environment should look like or become as the organization successfully implements its strategies and achieves its full potential. An organization may have to go through more than one cycle of strategic planning before it can develop an effective vision for itself; regardless, a full-blown vision of success is more likely to be a guide for strategy implementation than for strategy formulation.

Public value is the public and nonprofit sector equivalent of *shareholder value*. The idea of focusing on the importance of *creating public value* for public and nonprofit organizations was advocated by Mark H. Moore in his influential book *Creating Public Value: Strategic Management in Government* (1995). Public value is what the organization does, can, or should create that the public (or parts of it) values in a collective sense. The focus is on shared or collective benefits.

Possible Desired Implementation Outcomes

- A list of the implications for implementation found in the mandates, mission statement, values statement, and vision of success

- A set of performance indicators or assessment procedures for determining the extent to which the mandates are met, mission is fulfilled, values are observed, and vision is realized

Worksheet Directions

1. Someone should assemble in one spot the organization's mandates, mission statement, values statement, and vision of success. If these materials do not exist, then the implementation planning group should consider whether they should be created. Steps 2 and 3 in the companion workbook *Creating Your Strategic Plan*, third edition (Bryson & Alston, 2011), include worksheets that will help you prepare these documents. Note that conflicts may be found among the provisions of these documents: for example, some mandates may be at odds with the mission and values.

2. Fill out Worksheet 19 to gain clarity about the implications of the organization's mandates for implementation.

3. Fill out Worksheet 20 to understand more fully what the organization's mission means for implementation.

4. Worksheet 21 will help implementation planners discern what the organization's values imply for implementation efforts. Consider reviewing Worksheet 9 as well (or completing it now if it has not been used earlier) to assess how the organization's values relate to sustaining change and innovation.

5. Worksheet 22 will draw out the implications of the organization's vision of success for implementation.

6. Finally, Worksheet 23 will assist implementers in clarifying the public value that is created by the organization as it meets its mandates, fulfills its mission, lives its values, and realizes its vision.

WORKSHEET 19

Gaining Clarity About the Implications of the Organization's Mandates for Implementation

Instructions. Someone should take charge of assembling a list of the organization's formal and informal mandates. This list should be circulated to implementation team members in advance. Then the planning group should assemble and make use of this worksheet to draw out the implications of the mandates for the implementation process and for performance indicators that might be used to assess whether the mandates are being met.

Mandates are things the organization is required to do (or not do) and are often imposed by external actors. Mandates may be formal—such as laws, rules, or regulations—or informal—such as political mandates for change or deeply held public expectations. Mandates vary in what they require. Sometimes they require that a particular process or set of activities be followed; at other times they specify that a particular standard or outcomes be achieved. Sometimes they may need to be changed, if possible.

Mandate	Type of Mandate		What Does the Mandate Require Us to Do That Will Affect Implementation?	Performance Indicators to Measure Whether Mandate Is Met or Not	Assessment Process to Determine the Extent of Mandate Fulfillment
	Formal	**Informal**			

Understanding What the Organization's Mission Means for Implementation

Instructions. Someone should take charge of distributing the organization's current mission statement to implementation planning team members. Then the planning group should make use of this worksheet to draw out the implications of the mission for the implementation process and for performance indicators that might be used to assess whether the mission is being fulfilled.

A *mission statement* should succinctly capture the organization's purpose—its reason for existence. A mission statement should be action oriented and should articulate *what* the organization is here to do, and *why*. The statement also should say, in general, *how the organization will pursue its work* in order to create lasting and significant public value.

Mission Aspect	How Does or Should This Affect the Implementation Process?	Performance Indicators to Assess Whether the Mission Is Being Fulfilled or Not	Assessment Process to Determine the Extent of Mission Fulfillment
What does the mission say about *what* the organization exists to do?			

What does the mission say about *why* the organization should be doing what it does?			
What does the mission say about *how* the organization should pursue its work in order to create significant public value?			

WORKSHEET 21

Understanding What the Organization's Values Mean for Implementation

Instructions. Someone should take responsibility for distributing a copy of the organization's current values statement to all planning group members in advance of the meeting to discuss this statement and its implications for implementation. Then the planning group can use this worksheet to draw out the implications of the espoused values for the implementation process and identify performance indicators that might be used to assess whether the values are being observed.

Values form an important part of the foundation on which the organization operates. *Value statements* answer these questions: How do we want to conduct our business? How do we want to treat our key stakeholders? What do we really care about—that is, value? Values are a part of an organization's culture, so there may very well be a difference between the values people *espouse* and the values followed *in practice*.

What Are the Organization's Stated Values?	What Effect Should the Stated Values Have on the Implementation Process?	What, if Any, Are the Discrepancies Between Stated Values and Values in Practice, and How Might They Be Addressed?	Performance Indicators to Assess Whether Values Are Being Observed	Assessment Process to Determine the Extent of Value Observance

WORKSHEET 22

Understanding What the Organization's Vision of Success Means for Implementation

Instructions. A copy of the organization's vision of success should be distributed to implementation planning team members prior to their meeting. Then the planning group should gather and make use of this worksheet to draw out the implications of the vision of success for the implementation process and to identify performance indicators that might be used to assess whether the vision has been realized. Some aspects of this worksheet may already have been covered in Worksheets 19, 20, and 21. This worksheet should be used to address topics not dealt with previously.

An organization's vision statement—often called a *vision of success*—typically describes what the organization and key parts of its external environment should look like or be as the organization successfully implements its strategies and achieves its full potential. An organization may have to go through more than one cycle of strategic planning before it can develop an effective vision for itself, which means that many organizations will not have developed all the items listed on this worksheet prior to implementation. When that is the case, the planning team should do what it can now and also make a note that it might be advisable to come back later and complete the rest of the worksheet. A full-blown vision of success is more likely to be a guide for strategy implementation than for strategy formulation, but implementation does not have to wait for a full-blown vision of success to be prepared.

Complete visions of success will probably detail the following organizational attributes:

· Vision of how the world will be improved by the organization and its work. Changes the organization seeks in its external environment are likely to be described: for example, fewer families in poverty, lower crime rates, greater school readiness, and so on.

· Mission

· Basic philosophy, core values, and cultural characteristics

· Goals, if they have been established

· Basic strategies

· Performance criteria (such as critical success factors)

· Important decision-making rules

· Ethical standards expected of all employees

Vision Element	What Does the Vision Element Require Us to Do or Imply That We Should Do That Will Affect Implementation?	Performance Indicators to Measure Whether the Vision Is Being Realized in Practice	Assessment Process to Determine the Extent to Which the Vision Is Being Realized in Practice
Statement of how the world will be improved by the organization and its work			
Mission			
Basic philosophy, core values, and cultural characteristics			
Goals			

Worksheet 22

Implementing and Sustaining Your Strategic Plan. Copyright © 2011 by John Wiley & Sons, Inc. All rights reserved.

Basic strategies				
Performance criteria, such as critical success factors				
Important decision-making rules				
Ethical standards expected of all employees				
Changes in the external environment that the organization is trying to produce				

Worksheet 22

Implementing and Sustaining Your Strategic Plan.

WORKSHEET 23

How and Why the Organization Creates Public Value

Instructions. *Public value* is the public and nonprofit sector equivalent of *shareholder value*. The idea of focusing on the importance of *creating public value* for public and nonprofit organizations was advocated by Mark H. Moore in his influential book *Creating Public Value Strategic Management in Government* (Cambridge, MA: Harvard University Press, 1995). Public value is what the organization does, can, or should create that the public (or parts of it) values in a collective sense. The focus is on shared or collective benefits.

Review Worksheets 19, 20, 21, and 22, and then respond to the following questions:

1. What *public value*—meaning publicly available, shared, or collective benefits—does our organization create or strive to create?

2. How does our mission point to the creation of public value?

3. How do our mandates help (or hinder) the creation of public value?

4. How do our values help (or hinder) the creation of public value?

5. How does our vision of success focus on the creation of public value?

6. Why should we care about what public value we create?

7. What is our short explanation (*elevator speech*) about what we do to create public value and why it matters? (Note that Worksheet 56 focuses directly on creating an elevator speech. This question helps prepare implementers to fill out that worksheet.)

Comments:

Worksheet 23

Getting Clear About Strategies That Will Continue, Will Be Started, or Will Be Phased Out

Purpose of Step

The purpose of Step 6 is to sharpen understanding of the organization's exact priorities among existing strategies (or parts of strategies) that will continue, new strategies that are outlined in the strategic plan, and strategies that are to be phased out. Strategic plans typically focus on what is desired that is new, and they often remain vague about what will continue and what, if anything, will stop. Gaining clarity about what will stop is important because the resources that are freed by the *stop agenda* may be needed to continue strategies or start new ones.

Possible Desired Implementation Outcomes

- Clarity about the organization's priorities among existing strategies, programs, products, services, and projects

- Clarity about the priority to be attached to proposed new strategies, programs, products, services, and projects

- Creation of an agenda of strategies, programs, products, services, and projects that are to be phased out

- Reasonably detailed specification of all existing and new strategies to actually be implemented

Worksheet Directions

1. Clearly document your organization's existing strategic, program, service, and project priorities, using Worksheet 24. An understanding of what the

organization is currently doing is the starting point for the effective integration of ongoing operations and any new priorities identified in the strategic plan. In order to adequately resource and implement higher-level priorities spelled out in the strategic plan, the organization likely will need to shift some (and conceivably all) of its efforts and resources from what it is currently doing to those new, higher-level priorities.

2. Using Worksheet 25, assess the strategic plan's strategic, program, service, and project priorities.

3. Then use Worksheet 26 to reconcile the organization's current activities with those envisioned in the strategic plan.

4. For each existing strategy that will continue and each new strategy developed through the strategic planning process, develop a clear strategy statement and a list of the key elements of the strategy (Worksheet 27). The organization's resource situation and mandates may make a phased approach to the implementation of the strategic plan necessary.

5. In Step 11, action plans will be developed for each existing strategy that is kept, each new strategy that is pursued, and each strategy that is being phased out (that is, there should be action plans for implementing the stop agenda). Operational and administrative personnel should be involved in developing these plans. Action plans must be carefully coordinated and tied to the strategy statements developed using Worksheet 27.

Evaluating Priorities for Existing Strategies, Programs, Products, Services, and Projects

Instructions. Use as many copies of this worksheet as necessary to evaluate the priority of each existing strategy, program, product, service, and project.

Existing Strategies, Programs, Products, Services, Projects	Criteria for Establishing Priority, Including (at Least) Impacts on Mandates, Mission, Key Stakeholders, and Organization; Ability to Deliver Desired Outcomes	Priority (low, moderate, or high)	Resources Used			Time Frame
			People	Financial	Other Resources	

Evaluating Priorities for Proposed New Strategies, Programs, Products, Services, and Projects

Instructions. Use as many copies of this worksheet as necessary to evaluate the priority of each proposed strategy, program, product, service, and project.

Proposed Strategies, Programs, Products, Services, Projects	Criteria for Establishing Priority, Including (at Least) Impacts on Mandates, Mission, Key Stakeholders, and Organization; Ability to Deliver Desired Outcomes	Priority (low, moderate, or high)	Resources Used			Time Frame
			People	Financial	Other Resources	

Reconciling Priorities Among Existing and Proposed Strategies, Programs, Products, Services, and Projects

Instructions. Using Worksheets 24 and 25, compile a master list of priorities that reconciles the organization's current strategies, programs, products, services, and projects with those proposed in the strategic plan.

Existing Priorities That Should Be Retained (strategies, programs, products, services, projects)	Strategic Plan Priorities That Should Be Pursued (strategies, programs, products, services, projects)

Existing Priorities That Should Be Phased Out (strategies, programs, products, services, projects)	Strategic Plan Priorities That Should Not Be Pursued at This Time (strategies, programs, products, services, projects)

Worksheet 26

WORKSHEET 27

Strategy, Program, Product, Service, or Project Statement and Component Elements

Instructions. Fill out a separate strategy statement and component elements worksheet for each strategy, program, product, service, or project. The list of questions is lengthy, but it's important to answer them because they draw out important elements and aspects of implementing a strategy, program, product, service, or project.

1. Strategy, program, product, service, or project name:

2. The strategy, program, product, service, or project can or should be treated as

   ☐ A fairly discrete set of easily implemention activities that do not need to be organized into a project

   ☐ A single project

   ☐ Part of a program consisting of more than one project and other work

   ☐ Part of an even larger collection of projects or programs that are grouped together with other work to improve their management and to achieve strategic objectives

   ☐ Other (specify):

3. What is the purpose of the strategy, program, product, service, or project?

4. What are the goals (or intended results or outcomes) of the strategy, program, product, service, or project?

5. What performance measures are being or should be used to measure goal achievements, results, or outcomes?

6. Which stakeholders must be satisfied according to their criteria for satisfaction? (Check their criteria for satisfaction against the list of performance measures in the responses to question 5 and to Worksheets 19, 20, 21, and 22, and reconcile, if necessary.)

Stakeholders Who Must Be Satisfied for the Strategy, Program, Product, Service, or Project to Be Successfully Implemented	Their Criteria for Satisfaction

Worksheet 27

Implementing and Sustaining Your Strategic Plan.

7. What is the theory behind the strategy, program, product, service, or project? What makes people believe it will work to achieve the goals, do well against the performance indicators, and satisfy key stakeholders according to their criteria for satisfaction?

8. What are the principal components of the strategy, program, product, service, or project, and how do they address the issue(s) that prompted it and achieve the goals? Consider the following:

- Main components or features (key building blocks) of the strategy, program, product, service, or project:

- Necessary capabilities or competencies:

- Timetable for implementation, including any phase-in requirements (such as prototyping, pilot projects, demonstration projects, phase-in by geographical area, and so forth):

- Organization(s) or part(s) of organization(s) involved and persons responsible at present for implementation:

Organization(s) or Part(s) of Organization(s) Involved	Persons Responsible
Whole organization:	
Department(s):	
Division(s):	
Unit(s):	
Function(s):	
Program or project office:	
Other organizations:	
Other external stakeholders:	

Worksheet 27

Implementing and Sustaining Your Strategic Plan.

- Resources required—financial and otherwise—for staff, facilities, equipment, partners, contractors, volunteers, service recipients, training and development, and so on. List all resources needed and attach financial costs where possible:

- Total costs for start-up, annual operating costs, capital costs, and overall costs for the projected life of the strategy:

- Estimated savings, if any, over present approaches:

Worksheet 27

Implementing and Sustaining Your Strategic Plan.
Copyright © 2011 by John Wiley & Sons, Inc. All rights reserved.

- Flexibility or adaptability of strategy, program, product, service, or project:

- Effects on other organizations, departments, persons, or communities:

- Effects on other strategies, programs, products, services, or projects:

- Rule, policy, or statutory changes required:

- Procedures for *debugging* the strategy, program, product, service, or project during implementation—that is, *formative evaluation* plans (M. Q. Patton, *Utilization-Focused Evaluation*, 4th ed. [Thousand Oaks, CA: Sage, 2008]):

- Arrangements for subsequent evaluations to see whether or not the strategy, program, product, service, or project has worked—that is, *summative evaluation* (M. Q. Patton, *Utilization-Focused Evaluation*, 4th ed. [Thousand Oaks, CA: Sage, 2008]):

- Associated risks and how they might be managed:

- Other important features:

Worksheet 27

Implementing and Sustaining Your Strategic Plan.

- Summary of requirements for implementation success:

9. Which stakeholders and aspects of stakeholder relationships are crucial for effective implementation of the strategy, program, product, service, or project?

Stakeholder	Crucial Aspects of Relationship

Worksheet 27

Implementing and Sustaining Your Strategic Plan.
Copyright © 2011 by John Wiley & Sons, Inc. All rights reserved.

Resourcing and Structuring Implementation, Alignment, and Ongoing Learning

4

Resourcing Implementation

Step 7: Budgeting the work

Step 8: Creating an implementation management structure

Step 9: Developing effective implementation teams

Step 10: Organizing alignment and learning processes

Step 11: Putting it all together in strategy maps and action plans

Step 7

Budgeting the Work

Purpose of Step

The purpose of Step 7 is to align the strategies the organization is or will be pursuing with resources, especially financial and people resources. This means making sure needed resources are available for strategies that continue and are also available for new strategies identified in the plan. What gets paid for and staffed gets done. An organization's budgeting process thus should reconcile strategic priorities determined in Step 6 with the day-to-day operating costs and activities envisioned by those priorities, as well as with capital costs. Completing Step 7 often involves the implementation coordinating committee (ICC), sponsors, champions, managers, and budget specialists throughout the organization.

We must reemphasize that if an organization is not able to fund a significant part of its high-priority implementation agenda, then it probably should not have been doing strategic planning. But we also emphasize that not all *new* strategies and actions need *new* funding; instead, funds can often be shifted around if the organization has the will to do so. Stopping doing things that involve established funding arrangements, personnel, and coalitions of support is not easy. The implementation sponsors, champions, ICC, and other key stakeholders may well have to work hard to make important funding shifts happen, along with related personnel and stakeholder relationship adjustments.

Many organizations will need to alter their budgeting processes and cultures to support budgeting *what needs to be done* as a result of the plan in place of budgeting *what has always been done*. In other words, in many organizations, instead of strategic planning driving the budget, the budget comes first. Consequently, what was already in the budget gets a pass, and the planning then focuses mainly on how to implement what was already in the budget. Strategic planning is reduced to *strategic programming* because the strategies are already given (Mintzberg, 1994). There is little room in such organizations for new strategies or strategic initiatives. In contrast, organizations that take a proactive, budget-the-plan approach to resource allocation are better able to align strategic planning, budgeting, and operations and thus make the move to *strategic management*, in which strategic planning and implementation are integrated. Integrating the two is where the rubber meets the road—where funding for strategies, programs, products, services, projects, and the staffing they need occurs—and new strategies and initiatives get the resources they need, or they don't.

149

An important part of strategic management thus involves creating a financial management system and budget that includes and aligns

- Strategic initiatives, including stopping some things
- Ongoing day-to-day program operations
- Capital funding for fixed assets

Proactive budgeting and careful integration (as needed) of any new strategic initiatives into the existing funded programs will help ensure that the daily work of the organization is aligned with the organization's strategic goals.

One way to bridge any undesirable planning-budgeting divide is to be sure to involve budget managers and staff in the strategic planning process and on implementation recommendation and action teams, or I-Teams (discussed in Step 9). Their knowledge of the budget, financial flows, and guiding rules and regulations can be invaluable. In addition, our experience is that the budget team can often uncover ways to get something resourced that are not apparent to others—or conversely, if not effectively engaged, can raise barriers to plan implementation.

A great deal of practical guidance is available on how to prepare budgets. The Government Finance Officers Association, for example, offers a wealth of information and publications relevant to public budgeting that is also useful for nonprofit organizations (http://www.gfoa.org). The worksheets in this step provide templates that will help implementers develop budgets linked to strategic priorities. The worksheets will also help implementers finalize a stop agenda of those things the organization will no longer do in order to ensure adequate resources for the new things it has decided to do.

Possible Desired Implementation Outcomes

- Creation of a strategically managed budgeting system that gives explicit attention to

    a. Funding already existing strategies that will continue

    b. Funding new strategic initiatives

    c. Integrating ongoing operations with continuing and new strategies

    d. Phasing out funding for items on the stop agenda

    e. Capital funding for fixed assets

- As a step toward the first desired outcome, creation of a budget and budget process that marshals adequate resources to fund priority strategic work and related day-to-day operations

- Detailed information on the funds required for existing and new strategies and initiatives

- Detailed identification of the annual funds required to address each strategic goal
- Detailed identification of funds recovered from programs, products, services, and projects that are being phased out
- Clarity about the fiduciary oversight roles of key members of the organization, including the ICC, sponsors, and champions

Worksheet Directions

1. Use Worksheet 28 for guidance in developing a budget for implementation for each strategic initiative or project. This worksheet will help implementers and decision makers to understand the actual costs attributable to pursuit of each strategic initiative.

2. Consider using an appropriately modified version of Worksheet 29 to develop a summary budget—a big-picture view—for implementation, showing the costs of all strategic initiatives or projects.

3. Large and complex organizations may find it useful to use Worksheet 30 to develop a summary annual budget for implementation, showing the costs by project, program (multiple related projects), and portfolio (related projects and programs) and also overall. Again, the point is to develop a big-picture view of the costs of implementation, especially if those costs can be tied to strategic goals. It may also make sense to create a multiyear version of this worksheet.

WORKSHEET 28

Developing a Budget for Strategic Plan Implementation

Instructions. Complete a copy of the worksheet that follows for *each* strategy or strategic initiative (program, product, service, or project) to show the estimated costs of pursuing it for inclusion in the budget. Keep fine-tuning the worksheet and the budget as more information becomes available. Remember that a budget is just a planning tool and a set of estimates. Get any assistance needed to fill out the worksheet. Involve the organization's budget personnel in providing assistance, options, and advice. They need to integrate and manage implementation budget requests within the organization's overall budget and often must defend the requests to management and outside oversight authorities.

Present the worksheets to management and any related implementation recommendation and action team (I-Team). Keep the communications open, and accept modifications that improve the information in the worksheet.

Project name/title/number: _____

Tasks or phases: _____

Priority: High _____ Moderate _____ Low _____

Estimated timeline:

Short-term _____ Midterm (annual) _____ Long-term (multiyear) _____

1. Resources needed:

   • Total funding needed (per year and overall): _____

      Budgeted: _____

      New funds: _____

      Reallocation of existing funds: _____

Capital funds: _____

- People needed:

Management: _____

_____

Operational: _____

_____

Functional (such as budget and finance, IT, HR): _____

_____

2. Other resources (facilities, overhead, equipment, travel, consultants, training and professional development, and so on):

_____

_____

_____

_____

_____

_____

_____

Worksheet 28

Implementing and Sustaining Your Strategic Plan.
Copyright © 2011 by John Wiley & Sons, Inc. All rights reserved.

3. Effect on other initiatives or projects:

4. Desired or expected outcomes:

5. Estimated benefits (or public value created):

WORKSHEET 29

Developing a Summary Budget for Implementation

Instructions. Complete the worksheet below to show the estimated costs of pursuing all of the strategic implementation initiatives or projects. Again, involve the organization's budget staff, and keep fine-tuning the budget as more information becomes available. Project budgets may be grouped into program budgets (where a program consists of a related set of projects) for ease of understanding and management. Also, it may be useful to include more categories of information than shown below; for example, the specific *strategic goal* or *strategy* addressed by each project or group of projects, the desired outcomes, and so forth.

Example of Strategic Project Summary Budget					
Project	**Budget and Sources (for example, budgeted, new funds, reallocated, capital funds)**	**Priority**	**Project Leader**	**Timeline (from start to finish of project)**	**Status**
Project A	$$$$$	H	Smith	2011	Started
Project B	$$$$$	M	Jones		(TBD)
Project C	$$$$	H	(TBD)		Pending
Project D	$$$$$				
TOTAL	$$$$$$				

Strategic Initiative or Project Summary Budget					
Initiative or Project	**Budget and Sources (for example, budgeted, new funds, reallocated, capital funds)**	**Priority**	**Project Leader**	**Timeline (from start to finish of project)**	**Status**

Worksheet 29

Implementing and Sustaining Your Strategic Plan.

Developing a Strategic Annual Budget for Large, Complex Organizations

Instructions. Complete this matrix to show the full annual costs of pursuing each strategic goal. Be sure to include costs for all standard categories, including staff, training and professional development, facilities, consultants, evaluation and reporting, overhead, equipment, travel, capital costs, and so on.

Strategic Goal	Strategic Portfolios of Work for Each Strategic Goal					
	Program Costs	Costs of Projects Not Part of a Program	Program and Project Total Costs	Capital Costs	Costs of Strategy Elements or Initiatives Distinct from Programs, Projects, and Capital Costs	Total Annual Cost of Pursuing Each Strategic Goal (that is, costs of results)
Strategic Goal #1	Program:					
	• Project #1					
	• Project #2					
	• Project #3					

Strategic Goal #2	Program:		
	• Project #4		
	• Project #5		
Strategic Goal #3	Program:		
	• Project #6		
	• Project #7		
	• Project #8		
Strategic Goal #4	Program:		
	• Project #9		
	• Project #10		

Total annual cost of strategic priorities (that is, the sum of the costs of the strategic portfolios of work): _____

Worksheet 30

Implementing and Sustaining Your Strategic Plan. Copyright © 2011 by John Wiley & Sons, Inc. All rights reserved.

Creating an Implementation Management Structure

Purpose of Step

The purpose of Step 8 is to help organizations create an implementation management structure and set of related management processes that will facilitate bringing to life the strategies that emerge from the strategic planning effort. The basic idea is that organizational structures and processes should be *designed to help*—rather than hinder—strategy implementation and goal achievement. The basic starting premise is that *structure should follow strategy* (although the relationship between structure and strategy is actually reciprocal, as described in the next paragraph). An organization's existing governance, line management, functional, and operational structure and personnel complements should be used to the extent they can be to facilitate implementation of strategies, strategic initiatives, programs, projects, and so on, that emerge from the strategic planning effort. If the existing organizational structure is not able to handle the change management work that goes with implementing this strategic agenda, it should itself be changed or implementation success will suffer. For example, a newly adopted strategy may suggest that an organization stop providing a specific program or service and shift money to a higher priority need. This change may mean the organization should change its structure by eliminating or modifying an organizational unit or redesigning a division, bureau, or department.

Existing structures will clearly affect what strategies are viable in the short run. In most cases, existing structures will make some strategies easier to implement than others; in other cases, existing structures may make it harder or even impossible to implement particular strategies. So Mintzberg, Ahlstrand, and Lampel (2009, pp. 37–38) have it right when they say, "structure follows strategy the way the left foot follows the right in walking. In effect, strategy as well as structure both support the organization as well as each other. Each always precedes the other, and follows it, except when the two move together. . . . Strategy formation is an integrated process, not an arbitrary sequence." A rich dialogue involving key decision makers and operations personnel thus should be sought in order to determine how best to use or change existing structures to support implementation of the

159

strategies decided on in Step 6. But recognize as well that most strategies can never be fully specified in advance, and organizational structures are always being adapted to new circumstances and learning.

Previous steps in the Implementation Change Cycle should have led to an understanding and decisions about many of the elements of an effective implementation management structure and process. Some elements were probably given to begin with; some were decided in Steps 1 through 7, and still others are yet to come. Step 8 is intended to align management structures and processes into a coherent implementation management system and to establish placeholders for things yet to be decided. Things already decided upon may include

- The role of decision-making bodies, such as cabinets, boards of directors, or elected councils
- Who the implementation sponsors are (Step 2)
- Who the implementation champions are (Step 2)
- The role and membership of an implementation coordinating committee (ICC) (Step 2)
- An understanding of what works and what doesn't when it comes to organizational change (Step 3)
- Clarification of key stakeholders and their roles (Step 4)
- The effects on implementation of mandates, mission, vision, and values and the important performance indicators linked to each (Step 5)
- Clarity regarding the nature and content of strategies to be implemented (Step 6)
- Development of budgets for the work to be done (Step 7)

With these elements of an implementation management structure and process in place, it may be possible to implement many new strategies or parts of strategies with relatively little effort or reorganization. For example, some kinds of rule changes, alterations in fundraising emphases, creation of new outreach strategies, or simple process management improvements may not require organizational change. It should be possible to assign the tasks and adequate resources to someone or a small group to take action and to report back when it is completed (see Worksheet 53). But other kinds of strategies or parts of strategies may require a great deal more effort, resources, and reorganization. Here is where projects, programs, and portfolios come into play as tools to manage these strategies. All three may be distinguished from ongoing *operations*, which may be defined as "permanent endeavors that produce repetitive outputs, with resources assigned to do basically the same sets of tasks according to the standards institutionalized in a product [or service] life cycle" (Project Management Institute, 2008, p. 12).

Projects, programs, and portfolios are initiatives or groups of initiatives varying in scope and undertaken to improve operations (see Figure 7). *Projects* are the most discrete and are temporary endeavors undertaken to produce a specific product, service, or other result. Examples include repairing the potholes in a town after a hard winter, undertaking a fundraising event, installing computers in an office, or building an overpass. They are temporary by nature and have a finite time frame for completion, with start and finish dates, and usually have predefined objectives or desired outcomes. They typically involve a number of people with specific knowledge, skills, and abilities pulled together on an as-needed basis and given a specific

FIGURE 7

Portfolios, Programs, and Projects

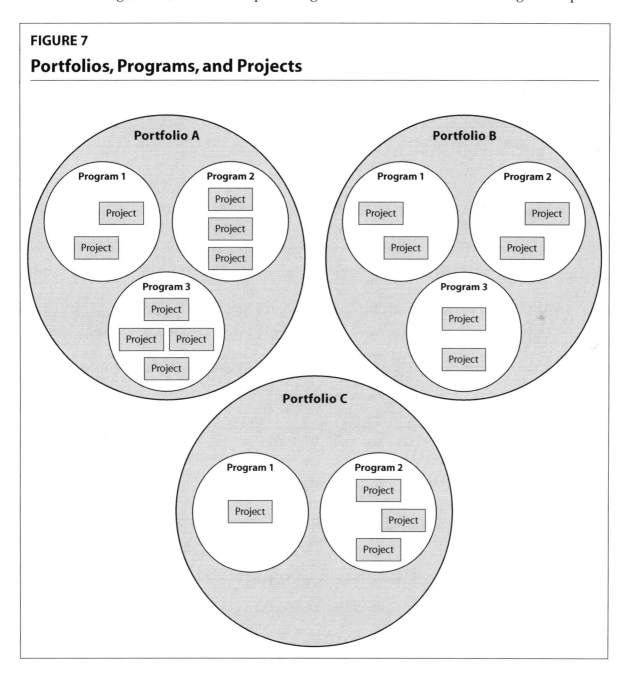

set of resources with which to work under the direction of a *project manager*. The project can usually be broken down into a set of phases, major tasks, and subordinate activities and can be controlled by an authorized scope and set of constraints, including specified purposes, allocated resources, staff complements, and so on. Finally, projects typically go through phases of initiation, planning, executing, monitoring and controlling, and closing (Project Management Institute, 2008, p. 6).

Programs are "a group of one or more related projects managed in a coordinated way to obtain benefits and control not available from managing them as separate individually" (Project Management Institute, 2008, p. 9). For example, while repairing a town's potholes after a hard winter will probably be a project, road repair in general will probably involve a program or work in the town's department of public works. For another example, a fundraising event put on by an organization will be a project, whereas fundraising in general will involve a program of work. Programs may also include elements of related work outside the scope of the discrete projects in the program. (Note that a project may or may not be part of a program, but a program will always have one or more projects.) Programs typically have longer time frames than projects. Programs thus involve more complex oversight and management than specific projects. A *program manager* is typically in charge of a program area and, in larger organizations, often has management teams leading the various projects in a program area. Because programs are typically bigger in scale and have larger resource requirements than projects, they are often more formally adopted, funded, and monitored by the organization's most senior managers and policymakers than many projects are.

Portfolios are usually an even larger collection of projects or programs that are grouped together with other work both to facilitate effective management of that work and to achieve strategic objectives. Portfolios might be created, for example, to help the organization manage major infrastructure, technology, fiscal management, or capital management efforts. A *portfolio manager* is typically in charge of two or more programs for the sake of improving organizational efficiency, cost effectiveness, and accountability. Portfolio managers often have several direct reports when the portfolio is large or complex.

Projects, programs, and portfolios all need to be managed effectively if they are to achieve their goals and objectives in a timely way and at reasonable cost and if their results are to be integrated effectively with ongoing operations.

Possible Desired Implementation Outcomes

- The identification and coordination of specific projects, programs, and portfolios of work to be undertaken to implement adopted strategies and achieve strategic goals and objectives

- Creation of project, program, and portfolio management implementation structures and related management processes

- Identification of management responsibilities and authority for these implementation structures and processes

- Streamlined and effective action planning

Worksheet Directions

1. Review all the filled-out copies of Worksheet 27, which identifies strategy, program, product, service, or project statements and component elements. For each specific element, fill out a copy of Worksheet 31, a project assignment worksheet. Note as well any additional work that is associated with a strategy, program, product, service, or project but that does not need to be organized as a project.

2. Review all the filled-out copies of Worksheets 27 and 31, paying particular attention to the responses to questions 1 and 2 on Worksheet 27. Then fill out Worksheet 32 by deciding what work goes into each column. Sponsors, champions, and the ICC are likely to be involved in deliberations about final choices in response to the following questions:

   a. Is there work that does not need to be organized as a project?

   b. Are there projects that should stand by themselves?

   c. Are there groups of projects and other work that should be organized into a program?

   d. And are there even larger collections of projects, programs, and other work that should be grouped into portfolios?

   Note that small organizations may have no, or very few, programs and no portfolios of work. Only large or very large organizations are likely to have multiple programs and portfolios of work.

3. Have a conversation about the appropriate organizational structure for managing and staffing the work. Depending on how the organization is already structured, the answer may be obvious. In other cases, some or even major reorganization may be necessary. In general, simpler organizational designs are preferable, as long as they actually facilitate getting the work done. In small organizations, really simple designs are likely the best choice (see, for example, Figure 8). In larger organizations, more complicated designs may be necessary (see Figures 9 through 11). Those involved in the deliberations should decide whether the work should be

   a. Assigned straight to sponsors of implementation teams who are led by a champion? (See Figure 8.)

FIGURE 8

ICC of Sponsors, Champions, and I-Teams

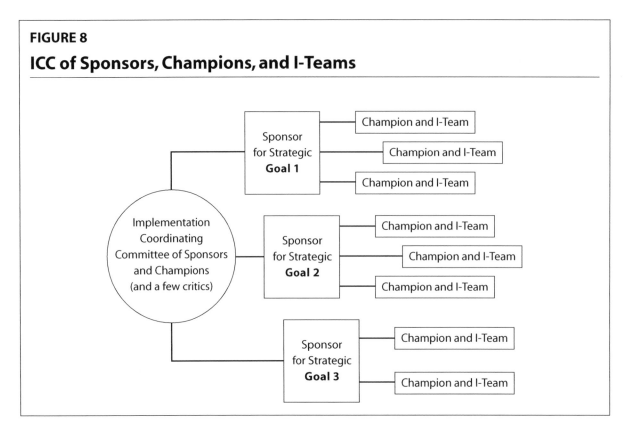

FIGURE 9

Functional Organization

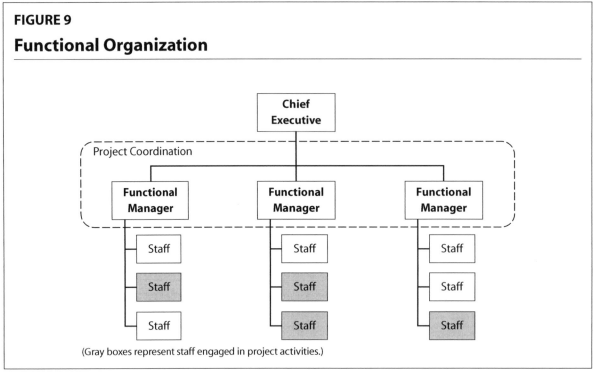

(Gray boxes represent staff engaged in project activities.)

Source: Project Management Institute. *A Guide to the Project Management Body of Knowledge (PMBOK® Guide).* Fourth Edition, Project Management Institute, Inc., 2008. Copyright and all rights reserved. Material from this publication has been reproduced with the permission of PMI.

FIGURE 10

Strong Matrix Organization

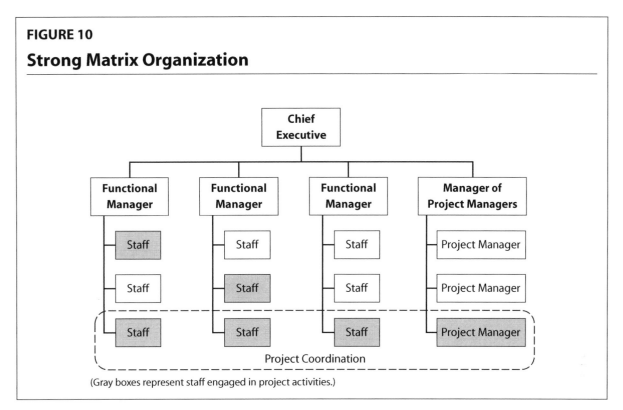

(Gray boxes represent staff engaged in project activities.)

Source: Project Management Institute. *A Guide to the Project Management Body of Knowledge (PMBOK® Guide)*. Fourth Edition, Project Management Institute, Inc., 2008. Copyright and all rights reserved. Material from this publication has been reproduced with the permission of PMI.

FIGURE 11

Projectized Organization

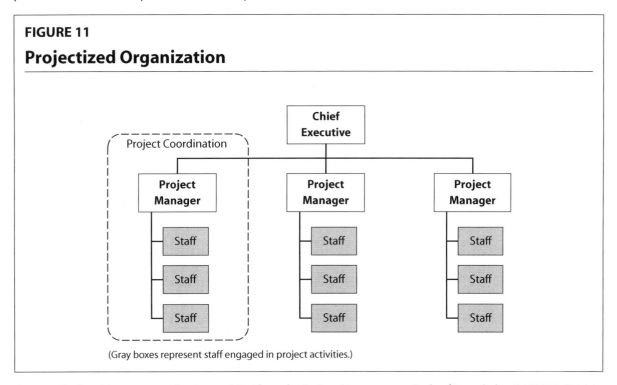

(Gray boxes represent staff engaged in project activities.)

Source: Project Management Institute. *A Guide to the Project Management Body of Knowledge (PMBOK® Guide)*. Fourth Edition, Project Management Institute, Inc., 2008. Copyright and all rights reserved. Material from this publication has been reproduced with the permission of PMI.

b. Assigned to existing functional line managers, who will then add project management responsibilities to their duties? Examples of functions that might be chosen are service delivery, finance, facilities management, and maintenance. (See Figure 9.)

c. Overseen by a project manager who draws on staff from functional departments, meaning that those staff will respond to dual authorities? This type of organization is referred to as a *matrix organization* because of the vertical and horizontal lines of authority and relationship. In a *strong matrix organization,* project management staff have considerable authority vis-à-vis functional management. (See Figure 10.)

d. Managed by a project manager who controls all of the necessary staff, meaning the organization is itself organized on a project basis? (See Figure 11.)

e. Set up as a hybrid version of Figures 8, 9, 10, and 11? See the Project Management Institute's *Guide to the Project Management Body of Knowledge* (2008, pp. 15–33), sometimes referred to as the PMBOK Guide, for a presentation and discussion of a variety of management structures that might work for project, program, and portfolio management.

4. Next, the group should have a conversation about the people who should be assigned responsibilities for any projects, programs, and portfolios and what their authority should be. After this discussion, fill out Worksheet 33. List key positions, responsibilities, authorities, and reporting relationships. Include specific persons' names where possible.

WORKSHEET 31

Project Assignment

Instructions. Fill out the following worksheet, being as specific as possible about names, dates, and amounts.

Project name: _____

Project contact: _____

Organizational unit: _____

Project priority: _____

1. What is to be done?

2. Who has the lead responsibility?

   • Project leader:

   • Team leaders (if any):

3. Who else needs to be involved?

   • From line management units:

   • From functional or staff units:

4. When will it be done?

   • Start date:

   • Milestones:

   • End date:

5. What resources are needed? Existing funding:

  • New funding:

  • Reallocated funding:

6. What are the expected results?

  • How will it be evaluated?

  • What are the success criteria?

7. What other projects are affected by this project, and what are the effects?

Assignment of Work to Project, Program, and Portfolio Categories

Instructions. Divide the organization's work among as many of the following categories as are applicable.

Easily Implemented Activities That Do Not Need to Be Organized into Projects	Projects	Programs (consisting of more than one project and other related work)	Portfolios (consisting of larger collections of projects or programs and related work)

WORKSHEET 33

Assignment of Projects, Programs, Portfolios, and Other Work

Instructions. Be as specific as possible in completing the following worksheet. Note that there are separate tables for projects, programs, and portfolios.

Project Name	Assigned to:	Responsibilities	Decision-Making Authority	Reporting Relationships
	☐ Functional manager: ☐ Project manager: ☐ Functional manager and project manager:			
	☐ Functional manager: ☐ Project manager: ☐ Functional manager and project manager:			
	☐ Functional manager: ☐ Project manager: ☐ Functional manager and project manager:			

Program Name	Assigned to:	Responsibilities	Decision-Making Authority	Reporting Relationships
	☐ Functional manager: ☐ Program manager: ☐ Functional manager and program manager:			
	☐ Functional manager: ☐ Program manager: ☐ Functional manager and program manager:			
	☐ Functional manager: ☐ Program manager: ☐ Functional manager and program manager:			

Worksheet 33

Implementing and Sustaining Your Strategic Plan.
Copyright © 2011 by John Wiley & Sons, Inc. All rights reserved.

Portfolio Name	Assigned to:	Responsibilities	Decision-Making Authority	Reporting Relationships
	☐ Functional manager: ☐ Portfolio manager: ☐ Functional manager and portfolio manager:			
	☐ Functional manager: ☐ Portfolio manager: ☐ Functional manager and portfolio manager:			
	☐ Functional manager: ☐ Portfolio manager: ☐ Functional manager and portfolio manager:			

Worksheet 33

Implementing and Sustaining Your Strategic Plan.

Step 9

Developing Effective Implementation Teams

Purpose of Step

The purpose of Step 9 is to put in place the competent *implementation recommendation and action teams* (or I-Teams) necessary for effective strategy and plan implementation. Teams are a basic implementation vehicle and a fundamental structure within which participation occurs, recommendations are developed for decisions by others, and actions are taken within authorized parameters. Teams are groups of people sharing a common purpose or goal and are particularly useful for completing complex tasks requiring the performance of many interdependent subtasks. Teams rely on members having knowledge, skills, and abilities that are complementary and thus offer the possibility of synergy through coordinated work. Often I-Teams include members from a variety of organizational units and therefore are a means for bridging a variety of disciplinary, structural, technical, service, and political boundaries. Ideally, the team allows each member to maximize his or her strengths and minimize his or her weaknesses in the service of a common goal.

The organization's strategic goals and the implementation work needing to be done should determine which I-Teams are needed and what their membership should be. I-Teams may include sponsors and often include champions. Sponsors and especially champions can provide the leadership and energy needed to keep a team inspired and mobilized in pursuit of the goals. The presence of a sponsor or champion can also facilitate alignment of the team's work with the organization's strategic goals. In some organizations, the implementation coordinating committee (ICC) delegates responsibility to its members to form the needed implementation teams. Another approach is to form temporary committees of the ICC to flesh out the implementation details and recommend implementation teams for each strategic goal or strategy. See Figure 8 in the previous step for one possible way of linking the ICC, sponsors, champions, and implementation teams.

Successful implementation teams have participation processes designed to

- Organize participation
- Create ideas for achieving strategic goals
- Build support for change

- Implement the changes for which the teams are authorized and responsible
- Build capacity and competence for the next round of strategic management work

Teams often need facilitation in order to do their best work. The facilitator role can be played by the team's leader, a team member, or the team as a whole, but sometimes an outside facilitator is needed. Facilitators (whether insiders or outsiders) can assist with four basic aspects of team functioning:

- Content or substance of the group's work
- Processes to be used
- Interactions within the group
- Logistics

When facilitators are used they should custom design an effective approach for working with the team that is based on both what the team needs to get done and the facilitator's own qualities and skills.

The worksheets that follow this step are designed to help implementers with building the needed teams, maintaining them, and disbanding them when the work is done. Several of the worksheets prompt individuals to assess how they and their team are doing and what improvements might be made. Many excellent resources are available that offer detailed information about useful tools and techniques to support effective teamwork (see, for example, Hackman, 2002; Johnson & Johnson, 2008).

Possible Desired Implementation Outcomes

- Needed I-Teams are identified and in place throughout the organization.
- Strategies and resources for team development are in place.
- Team and individual performance reviews are in place to guide implementation efforts, and a conscious effort is made to make ongoing learning and development a part of the team's work (see Step 10).
- Teams are disbanded when their specific strategic work is done (see Steps 11 and 12).
- The organization's capacity for future work is enhanced.

Worksheet Directions

1. Use Worksheet 34 to clarify who the members of an I-Team are and how their work relates to the organization's strategic goals. Make sure that the sum of the members' abilities and responsibilities is adequate for completing the task.

2. Once I-Teams have been formed, use an appropriately modified version of Worksheet 35 to clarify ICC and I-Team membership, roles and responsibilities, reporting relationships, and so on. (See also Worksheet 7.)

3. Worksheet 36 focuses on the team leader. (Feel free to revise the worksheet to fit your particular circumstances.) Have team leaders self-assess how they would respond to the questions. Then ask each leader to share his or her answers with someone who knows that leader well and to ask for feedback. Responses should be used by the team leader to improve his or her performance as needed.

4. Use Worksheet 37 to plan an agenda for each team meeting. The team leader or a designated team member should anticipate what the team expects to accomplish at a meeting. Agendas help team members to understand what results they are aiming toward. Whether an agenda is prepared in advance or on the spot, once the desired results are clear, the agenda can be further developed with time frames; more detail on the topics to be covered; and processes, tools, and techniques can be selected to best address each topic.

5. Exhibit 2 (which follows Worksheet 37) provides helpful advice on how to facilitate meetings. Each team member should be asked to read this advice prior to the first meeting, and the contents of this exhibit should be revisited periodically as part of assessing how well the team is functioning.

6. Worksheet 38 should be used to summarize each meeting, so that a record is kept and any necessary follow-up actions are noted and tracked. Meeting summaries are an important means of ensuring the accountability of the team and its individual members for the work to be done.

7. Meetings should be evaluated so that team members, individually and collectively, can assess how well they have done and what might be done to improve future meetings. Worksheet 39 provides a meeting evaluation form.

8. Teams should also periodically assess how well they are functioning and make any necessary or desirable improvements. Worksheet 40 offers a team self-assessment form. The results can inform an agenda for a dialogue about where the team does well, where it could do with some improvement, and what specific improvements might be made.

WORKSHEET 34

Creating Implementation Recommendation and Action Teams (I-Teams)

Instructions. This worksheet is designed to assist the implementation process sponsors and champions (and perhaps the ICC) decide who should be on an implementation recommendation and action team (I-Team). In small organizations, making these choices will be relatively easy, but in large or complex organizations, making suitable choices will take time, consultation with others, and careful consideration.

The first step in determining I-Team members is to make sure the implementation process sponsors and implementation process champions have a clear picture (often an actual graphic picture) of the organization, its structure, the key functions it performs, and its major personnel classifications (see Step 8). The second step is to gain clarity about the implementation agenda, including exactly what strategies are to be implemented and what major actions are to be taken. The sponsors and champions should use Worksheet 27 (and *Creating Your Strategic Plan* Worksheets 34, 35, 36, 37 and 38, if available; see Bryson & Alston, 2011) in the process of achieving this clarity. This information will then help guide determining who needs to be involved in the implementation process in order to ensure successful implementation of agreed strategies and actions. Implementation in organizations is greatly dependent on buy-in from employees at all levels and often other key stakeholders, so getting the right people on the I-Team is often vital to achieving success.

The sponsors and champions, along with perhaps the ICC and other key internal and external stakeholders, need to remind themselves: What are the most important things we are trying to achieve through the implementation process? What are the major strategies and bundles of related actions we are trying to implement? For each strategy an initial list of key components and tasks should be on hand. Note what is proposed to be done, when it should be done, who needs to be involved, what resources are needed, and how the elements contribute to successfully implementing strategic initiatives.

Strategy to be implemented: _____

1. What exactly is to be implemented? List major elements and accompanying actions to be taken to implement the strategy.

   -

   -

-

-

-

-

Comments:

2. In order for the strategy to be successfully implemented, which organizational units or groups across and up and down in the organization need to be involved?

    -

    -

-

-

-

Comments:

3. What major organizational functions (for example, service delivery, finance, communications, human resources, information technology, or administration) should be represented in this effort?

-

-

-

-

-

Comments:

4. Specifically, *who* should be considered for membership on the I-Team?

-

-

-

-

-

Worksheet 34

-

-

-

-

-

-

-

Comments:

Worksheet 34

Implementing and Sustaining Your Strategic Plan.

5. Does the previous list ensure that all major necessary job classifications (for example, managers to supervisory workers to line workers) are represented?

☐ Yes

☐ No

If no, which classifications are missing? Who might be considered who fits these classifications?

-

-

-

-

-

Comments:

6. Is representation from external stakeholders necessary (for example, from outside boards, unions, funders, or clients)?

☐ Yes

☐ No

If yes, which stakeholders should be involved?

-

-

-

-

-

Comments:

Implementing and Sustaining Your Strategic Plan.

7. Are all internal and external stakeholders with major concerns or likely to have such concerns represented?

    ☐ Yes

    ☐ No

    If no, who is missing?

    •

    •

    •

    •

    •

Comments:

8. Who should be involved to ensure that we have the organization's key functional knowledge areas, skills, and competencies represented? Who should be included who knows the organization's history and how to get things done? Who should be included who is a good communicator or is a key opinion leader or is politically well connected or is trusted by many or does really good work?

   •

   •

   •

   •

   •

Comments:

9. Keep adding names to the list. The results are to be kept confidential and are to be used by the organization's leadership, the implementation sponsors and champions, and the ICC to inform their selection of the I-Team.

10. In the final analysis, who should be on the I-Team?

    •

    •

    •

    •

    •

    •

    •

    •

    •

Worksheet 34

Implementing and Sustaining Your Strategic Plan.
Copyright © 2011 by John Wiley & Sons, Inc. All rights reserved.

WORKSHEET 35

ICC and I-Team Tasks, Membership, Competencies, Roles, and Responsibilities

Instructions. Modify this worksheet as necessary to fit your situation and clarify implementation coordinating committee (ICC) and implementation recommendation and action team (I-Team) tasks, membership, competencies, roles, and responsibilities.

Implementation Coordinating Committee

Members	Roles and Responsibilities	Reporting and Accountability Relationships

Strategic Goal #1	Charge/Task	Membership	Each Member's Knowledge Base and Competencies	Roles and Responsibilities	Dates of Operation	Reporting and Accountability Relationships
Team A						
Team B						
Team C						

Worksheet 35

Implementing and Sustaining Your Strategic Plan. Copyright © 2011 by John Wiley & Sons, Inc. All rights reserved.

187

Strategic Goal #2	Charge/Task	Membership	Each Member's Knowledge Base and Competencies	Roles and Responsibilities	Dates of Operation	Reporting and Accountability Relationships
Team A						
Team B						
Team C						

Worksheet 35

Implementing and Sustaining Your Strategic Plan. Copyright © 2011 by John Wiley & Sons, Inc. All rights reserved.

Strategic Goal #3	Charge/Task	Membership	Each Member's Knowledge Base and Competencies	Roles and Responsibilities	Dates of Operation	Reporting and Accountability Relationships
Team A						
Team B						
Team C						

Worksheet 35

Implementing and Sustaining Your Strategic Plan. Copyright © 2011 by John Wiley & Sons, Inc. All rights reserved.

189

WORKSHEET 36

Team Leader Self-Assessment

Instructions. Implementation teams have to address challenges and solve puzzles specific to their organization, task, responsibilities, and accountabilities. Team leaders should pay attention to group maintenance, task accomplishment, and member satisfaction.

Team leaders should answer the following questions as honestly as possible and then share their answers with someone who knows them well in order to get constructive feedback and to help develop a plan for self-improvement.

Category	Present			Future		
	Good	Average	Poor	Good	Average	Poor
1. I help the team set aggressive goals and motivate team members to break new ground, keeping the bar high when the going gets tough.						
2. I help the team engage in substantive dialogue.						
3. I mentor and coach team members.						
4. I make sure work gets assigned and overseen in appropriate ways.						
5. I work with the team to set timelines and expectations for work to be accomplished.						
6. I set and maintain a disciplined schedule for check-ins and evaluations.						
7. I hold myself and the team accountable for results.						
8. I remove barriers.						
9. I secure needed resources.						
10. I broker needed relationships, including with senior management and other key stakeholders.						
11. I am an effective spokesperson for the team.						

Comments:

Action plan for self improvement:

WORKSHEET 37

Meeting Agenda

Name of implementation team: _____

Date _____ Time: Start _____ End _____

Place of meeting: _____

Premeeting preparation (what to read, research, or prepare):

_____

_____

_____

Time	Topic/Task	Person Responsible	Objective and Expected Outcome (what the group is to know/discuss/create as a result)

Date of next meeting: _____

EXHIBIT 2

Tips for Facilitating a Meeting

The meeting facilitator's role is to design and manage a process that helps the team accomplish its work while also minimizing problems within the group. It is important to be attentive to meeting logistics (the room, seating, wall space, refreshments, restroom facilities, premeeting preparation, and so on), the content (substance) of meeting topics, and the interaction (process) of the team members. The meeting facilitator—who may be the team leader, a team member, or an outside facilitator—and team members share responsibility for progressing toward the goals of the team. The facilitator serves as a guide to the team for a range of activities, including the following.

Interaction (process)
- Resolving conflicts
- Monitoring or encouraging participation
- Exploring reactions and feelings
- Keeping the members focused on the meeting objectives
- Managing time

Topic Content (substance)
- Eliciting information, experience, attitudes, best practices
- Recording and analyzing data
- Generating alternatives
- Making decisions
- Developing future action plans
- Evaluating effectiveness

Facilitating Group Decisions
Facilitators often need to select processes to make group decisions. Making sound decisions while having thoughtful team participation is often a desirable goal. Employing appropriate processes and techniques will enable teams to make better and faster decisions. Team members will feel good about their involvement, and the overall effectiveness of the group will be enhanced. There is no magic technique that fits all situations. Matching decision-making processes (there are hundreds of excellent resources on decision making) to each particular situation is one of the arts of facilitation. Process techniques should be carefully selected before a team meeting. Here are some tips to help you facilitate a decision-making process that may be new to the meeting participants.

- Plan ahead so that you are very familiar with the process you intend to use.
- Explain the purpose of the process you use, in addition to giving specific instructions.
- Give specific instructions; when there are several steps, it will be helpful to provide them in writing.

- Clarify tasks when people are to fill certain roles, such as timekeeper, recorder, and the like.

- When a process is complete, restate the intended goals of the process so the participants understand what they did and what they gained from it.

Managing Group Interaction

From the beginning of a meeting it is important to establish a solid foundation for the way the team members will work together. Members need to know what is going to happen, feel they are in a safe environment, and trust others in order to fully participate in the meeting. They need to accept the role of the team leader or facilitator, agree to follow team ground rules, and be engaged actively in the work of the group.

Ground rules promote constructive team behaviors and are essential to keep the team on task and to promote a respectful meeting environment. A team leader might contribute ideas for ground rules; however, all members need to have an opportunity to contribute to the list. All team members should agree on the ground rules at the beginning of the team's work. It is helpful to post the ground rules during meetings to serve as a reminder of how the team has agreed to work. If someone violates the ground rules, it is the role of the team leader or other team members to draw attention to the behavior and remind the person of the rules. Ground rules are best when they are simple and enforceable.

Helping a group stay on track is an important role of a team meeting facilitator. The tendency for a team to wander and drift is a normal part of meetings. If the team wanders too much, however, the work does not get accomplished and team members lose interest. Levels of intervention range from doing nothing to forcefully directing the group. As a team wanders it is important to decide how gently or forcefully to intervene in the group process. Here are a few strategies you may consider when the team is not following its agenda or has identified so many additional agenda items that they will never fit into the allotted time.

- When you prepare an agenda prior to a meeting, be very conscious of not overloading the agenda. Consider that all agenda items need ample time for discussion, and then build in some additional time, knowing that items often take longer than expected.

- At the beginning of the team meeting, mention that one role you have is to keep the team on track. Say that you may interrupt the group if it appears the members are moving away from their stated purpose.

- When the team has too many items to address successfully in one meeting, ask members to identify two or three they want to focus on.

- At times it is appropriate to set time limits for discussion. Suggesting that team members limit their comments to a specific amount of time may also be used when there is a need to get input from several people or when a few people have been monopolizing the conversation.

- As you make suggestions to the group, explain how the team task accomplishment will be enhanced and how the team can benefit from the suggested changes in group process.

Source: Exhibit supplied by Sharon Roe Anderson.

Exhibit 2

Implementing and Sustaining Your Strategic Plan.

WORKSHEET 38

Meeting Summary

Date:_____

Meeting facilitator:_____ Recorder:_____

Attendees:_____

_____

_____

Action taken/decisions made:

1.

2.

3.

Notes regarding key points:

Subsequent Actions to Be Taken	Person Responsible	Expected Completion Date
Summarize meeting/distribute minutes		
Gather information/research a topic and report back		
Report to/brief someone/write briefing		
Seek input from someone		
Invite resource person(s) to future meeting		
Implement decision		
Update team work plan		
Other:		
Other:		
Other:		

Next meeting date: _____

Worksheet 38

WORKSHEET 39

Meeting Evaluation

Instructions. Meetings can be evaluated by the team leader, a visitor to the team, or by the team members. All can contribute to improving a meeting.

Meeting Evaluation by Team Members Responding Individually

1. To what extent did this meeting achieve the stated objectives?

Not at All   1   2   3   4   5   Completely

2. What was most helpful to you in advancing the work of the team?

3. What aspects were least helpful to you in advancing the work of the team?

4. Suggestions for improvement or other comments:

Meeting Evaluation by Team Members in a Group Discussion

1. How did we do in meeting our objectives for this meeting?

2. What can be done to improve our work together?

WORSHEET 40

Team Self-Assessment

Instructions. A challenge facing many implementation teams is neglect of their own growth—building their capacity. Often teams are deeply involved in the tasks and projects of their work, and having taken on additional responsibilities, there seems to be little time for learning and reflection. Use the following worksheet to rate your implementation team and then follow up with dialogue with the other team members regarding ways the team might improve.

Task Orientation	Good	Average	Poor
Members are clear about their purpose and goal.			
The team is able to focus on its work without distractions.			
Members collaborate, tapping talents and resources of all (knowledge, contacts, skills).			
Members represent the needed diversity of views and backgrounds, and team size is appropriate.			
Milestones are celebrated; achievement is recognized and rewarded.			
The team has a productive attitude, an inclination to hard work, and a willingness to overcome adversity.			
Members hold one another and the team as a whole accountable for completing work assigned in a high-quality and timely way.			

Comments:

Effective Communication and Conflict Management	Good	Average	Poor
Members listen to each other's views.			
Conflict is managed constructively rather than suppressed.			
Members have open and honest conversations.			
Members are compatible with one another and sensitive to their cultural differences.			

Comments:

Empowerment	Good	Average	Poor
Adequate opportunities are available and used for communication, shared decision making, and the flexibility exists for the team to solve its own problems.			
Individual members' roles are clear.			
Creativity is encouraged.			
Team norms support openness, sharing, mutual support, and cooperation.			
The team has effective strategies for obtaining needed resources, including time to work.			
Direction and support are tailored to members' needs.			

Comments:

Team Development	Good	Average	Poor
The team leader and others serve as coach and facilitator.			
Team responsibilities are shared.			
The team takes responsibility for its development and learning.			

Comments:

Worksheet 40

Implementing and Sustaining Your Strategic Plan.

Step 10

Organizing Alignment and Learning Processes

Purpose of Step

Recall that *strategy* is defined as the means by which an organization intends to accomplish a goal or objective. It summarizes a pattern across policies, programs, projects, decisions, and resource allocations. Getting *strategy alignment* right means making sure each strategy's pattern is a good one—as opposed to being uncoordinated (including with other strategies) and haphazard—based on the premise that better alignment will produce better organizational performance. Alignment has three different meanings and all are relevant to successful implementation. The first involves *arranging things in a line*, meaning there should be a direct connection all the way from mission to operations on the ground and the production of desired outputs and outcomes. The second meaning involves arranging and adjusting things so they are in a *proper relationship* to each other and therefore better coordination (including via effective conflict management) occurs. And the third means that individuals, groups, and organizations involved in implementation are essentially *in agreement* about what should be done, how, and why.

The purpose of Step 10 is to develop ways of ensuring that the various elements involved in implementing strategies are aligned from mission and mandates all the way to individual action plans and results. *Learning* is a central part of the alignment process, because alignment doesn't just happen—people have to learn how to make it happen. This means that various occasions and processes for learning must be designed into the implementation process. The outcome of the learning process should be changes in the organization or in its implementation process that lead to better alignment, better adaptation to changing circumstances, and improved capacity to pursue organizational purposes. Strategic management in this case becomes a kind of organizational development.

Learning is taking place all the time. But for *organizational learning* to occur, individuals, groups, and the organization itself must be involved (Crossan, Lane, & White, 1999). Individuals learn via intuiting and interpreting. Intuiting involves making use of experience, images, and metaphors. Interpreting involves making

203

use of language, cognitive maps, and conversation and dialogue. When the dialogue takes place in groups, the result can be integration via shared understanding, mutual adjustment of perceptions and interests, and fluidity in systems. Learning becomes institutionalized at the organizational level via agreed mission, vision, and values; agreed strategic and other plans, routines, rules, procedures, practices, and diagnostic systems; and ideally, enhanced capabilities for making desirable changes. A tension is created when new learning *feeding forward* from individuals to groups to the organization encounters the consequences of what was previously learned *feeding back* from the organization to groups to individuals. For example, institutional rules that were put in place for good reasons encounter resistance when their applicability is questioned because circumstances have changed. Dialogue and the resultant learning are important keys to managing this tension constructively.

Dialogue is central to learning. Dialogue and discussion are often used as synonyms, but they can be quite different. Discussion often involves one party trying to force his or her views on another party—a process not focused on the development of mutual understanding and commitment but on winning and losing. Listening in this case is typically not about appreciating what another says; instead, it simply means waiting one's turn, and often not politely. (Note that the suffix *-cussion* that appears in *discussion* also appears in *percussion* and *concussion*.) *Dialogue*, in contrast, is about really trying to understand what the other person is saying, enhancing creativity, and seeking common ground. It involves suspending judgment, not blindly defending one's view, and also using conflict constructively and staying with the process long enough to find good, mutually satisfactory answers. Dialogue is thus a central feature of effective conflict management.

Making dialogue a habit requires institutional support. Leaders should insist on dialogue when circumstances require it, and model it themselves by asking questions more than giving direction. The organization should also make a habit of using what Moynihan (2008) calls *learning forums*. These are defined as "routines that encourage actors to closely examine information, consider its significance, and decide how it will affect future action" (p. 19). Moynihan notes that learning is enhanced when there are multiple perspectives and different kinds of knowledge present and when power and status differences are minimized. These conditions are unusual in most hierarchies, and leaders must ensure that the standard practices of enforcing specialization and deferring to authority are suspended while the forum is in operation.

Dialogue and learning are also helped by making use of one or more of the many tools and techniques that assist idea representation, analysis, and synthesis. The repertoire of tools available in books and on the Web is huge; we mention just a few that are particularly useful: Step 11 includes guidelines for *strategy mapping*, but note that the basic mapping process can be used whenever understanding linkages among ideas is important (see also Bryson, Ackermann, Eden, & Finn, 2004; Bryson, 2011, Resource C). Resources A and B in this workbook include guidelines for, respectively, *brainstorming* and the *snow card* (or *affinity diagram*) technique. Many organizations make use of *logic modeling* to understand the theory behind what they are or should be doing, meaning the logic that links resources, activities, outputs, and intermediate and longer-term outcomes (see, for example, Knowlton & Phillips, 2008; McLaughlin & Jordon, 2010). *Business process mapping* is also a very useful implementation tool. It involves creating a map of exactly what a process actually is in practice, who is responsible at what point, and what results the process is achieving (or not). Once the current process has been clarified, it can often be improved significantly by setting a high standard, determining the requirements necessary to meet the standard, and refashioning the process to meet the requirements and achieve the standard (Deming, 1982; Hall & Johnson, 2009).

Formalized learning processes are also useful. The simplest may be Deming's (1982) famous Plan-Do-Check-Act cycle (also called the plan-do-study-act cycle, Deming cycle, or Shewart cycle). According to the American Society for Quality, the steps are as follows:

1. *Plan*. Recognize an opportunity and plan a change.

2. *Do*. Test the change. Carry out a small-scale study.

3. *Study*. Review the test, analyze the results, and identify what you've learned.

4. *Act*. Take action based on what you learned in the study step: If the change did not work, go through the cycle again with a different plan. If you were successful, incorporate what you learned from the test into wider changes. Use what you learned to plan new improvements, beginning the cycle again. [Reproduced by permission of Nancy R. Tague, *The Quality Toolbox, Second Edition* (Milwaukee: ASQ Quality Press, 2005). To order this book, visit ASQ at http://www.asq.org/quality-press.]

Formative evaluations are focused on program or project improvement, not on making summary judgments about effectiveness (which are typically called *summative evaluations*). Formative evaluations seek to understand what is going on in a program or project, analyze what is working and what is not, and feed back information and recommendations to implementers about how to improve it (see, for example, Fitzpatrick, Sanders, & Worthen, 2004; Patton, 2008).

Learning can also occur via performance reviews, coaching, and professional development. *Performance reviews* offer a kind of diagnostic control and professional development mechanism. *Coaching* involves focusing on an individual's or group's needs, accomplishments, and goals through close observation, and then providing helpful guidance on how to improve performance. *Professional development* includes constructive performance reviews and coaching, but there are many other approaches. Implementers should be aware of the desirability of linking individual and group professional development efforts to the implementation process. Implementation efforts themselves often provide significant on-the-job professional development, as long as necessary skill-building opportunities, learning forums, and reflection times are built into the process.

Possible Desired Implementation Outcomes

- Formal commitment to ongoing learning as an important part of the implementation process

- Clarification of what needs to be aligned

- Identification and design of necessary learning forums to help facilitate the learning and alignment; clarification about how the work of learning forums may be incorporated into practice

- Identification of formative evaluations that would be helpful

- Tying of performance reviews, coaching, and professional development to the implementation process and strategic goals of the organization

Worksheet Directions

1. The leadership of the implementation effort (policy board, ICC, and implementation sponsors and champions) should make a public commitment to the importance of building ongoing learning into the implementation process, build the infrastructure to support learning, and provide good models themselves of effective learners.

2. Use Worksheet 41 to understand more clearly what may need to be aligned and what might be involved in achieving necessary alignment.

3. Use Worksheet 42 to design necessary learning forums.

4. Worksheet 43 provides some suggestions and guidelines for engaging effectively in constructive dialogue. Have groups involved in implementation read this worksheet and revisit it if the occasion arises.

5. Use Worksheet 44 to identify needed formative evaluations.

6. Staff can use Worksheet 45 to have implementers individually self-assess performance and articulate areas for improvement and ways of doing so, perhaps prior to meeting with supervisors for a performance review. An optional companion assessment for supervisors to complete and discuss with individual employees is also included with this worksheet.

7. Worksheet 46 presents an option for an employee performance review form that includes attention to strategic goals.

8. Worksheet 47 is designed to help potential implementation coaches assess their skills and make plans for improvement.

9. Worksheet 48 can be used by individuals and groups to request professional development help. (Worksheet 40 helps teams assess their professional development needs.)

WORKSHEET 41

Alignment Checkup

Instructions. Alignment among implementation elements is typically assumed to be important based on the premise that better alignment will produce better organizational performance. Alignment involves:

- Arranging things in a line, meaning there should be a direct connection all the way from mission to operations on the ground and the production of desired outputs and outcomes.

- Arranging and adjusting things so they are in a proper relationship to each other and therefore better coordination occurs.

- Ensuring that individuals, groups, and organizations involved in implementation are essentially in agreement about what should be done, how, and why.

---

1. Consider having the ICC, implementation sponsors, implementation champions, or I-Team, or some combination of these, review the following implementation elements and decide whether they are in alignment or in need of adjustment.

Implementation Element	In Alignment	Needs Adjusting
Mission, vision, and values are shared.		
Mandates are known and followed—or changed when necessary.		
Strategic goals, objectives, and performance indicators support mission, vision, and values; are understood; and are shared.		
Effective leadership is in place: • Implementation coordinating committee • Sponsors • Champions • Implementation teams • Key stakeholders		

Attention is paid to planning and change efforts of the past and the lessons learned from them.		
Strategic work has adequate funding.		
Structures and processes to manage strategic work and facilitate implementation (including via effective conflict management) are in place.		
Strategy maps and action plans are available to help guide implementation.		
Strategic goals and operations are clearly and effectively linked.		
Mechanisms and practices are in place to facilitate ongoing learning that improves implementation effectiveness.		
Results of work (outputs and outcomes) are measured and evaluated and any necessary corrective actions are taken.		
Strategies for changing course are considered as needed.		

2. Based on the discussion, consider what should be done to increase alignment. Action plans and follow-up may be needed; Worksheets 49 through 53 offer guidance with this.

Worksheet 41

Implementing and Sustaining Your Strategic Plan.

Designing Learning Forums

Instructions. Learning forums are needed wherever it is important to examine information and explore its meaning and significance as a prelude to deciding what present or future action might be needed. Learning forums have the following characteristics (adapted from D. P. Moynihan, *The Dynamics of Performance Management: Constructing Information and Reform* [Washington, DC: Georgetown University Press, 2008], p. 179):

- They are routine, and not extraordinary, events and processes.

- Confrontations are avoided so as not to trigger defensive reactions.

- A collegial environment is established in which status and power differences are minimized.

- Participants include a diverse set of actors responsible for producing useful knowledge and recommendations.

- Dialogue is the norm, and the dialogue is focused on how to achieve organizational goals, meet the mandates, and fulfill the mission.

- Assumptions are identified and closely examined, perhaps even suspended for the sake of argument.

- Quantitative information and knowledge are used to the extent possible, including what is known in relation to goals, issues, outputs, outcomes, strengths and weaknesses, comparisons and contrasts, and baselines.

- Experiential knowledge about how things are working (or not) is welcomed.

Note that meetings of standing groups can be learning forums, as when school boards alternate study sessions (learning forums) with decision-making sessions.

To begin identifying and designing your learning forums, answer the following questions.

1. At what places in the implementation process and levels in the organization is it necessary or desirable to have ongoing learning forums?

2. Which already existing groups can serve as learning forums for some of the work?

3. What new learning forums will be needed? What will each of them focus on?

4. Who will convene each forum?

5. What kind of training will be needed to help the forum embody the characteristics of effective learning groups?

6. What is the process by which learning will be translated into advice?

7. How will the effectiveness of learning forums be evaluated?

8. How will the work of learning forums be acknowledged and celebrated?

Worksheet 42

Implementing and Sustaining Your Strategic Plan.

WORKSHEET 43
Facilitating Dialogue Guidelines

Instructions. Have members of any group wishing to engage in a dialogue about important matters read this worksheet and then use it as a set of guidelines and also as a way to assess how well the dialogue is being managed by the group and what might be done to improve the dialogue.

Dialogue is an important way of fostering learning because learning at its best involves exploring many possible problem definitions and possible problem solutions before settling on how best to look at a problem and what to do about it. Learning at its best thus embraces both divergent and convergent thinking: divergent when many possibilities are being considered and convergent when choices of problem definitions and solutions are made.

Dialogue fosters learning by deliberately slowing down the group process in order to save time in the end by solving the right problem in the right way. In other words, it can take very little time to misdiagnose a problem and jump to solutions. That may look efficient on the front end, but may be very inefficient indeed on the back end when you have solved the wrong problem or even solved the right problem but in the wrong way. Dialogue is thus a crucial feature of effectively managing conflict in the present and avoiding unnecessary conflict in the future.

What Is Dialogue?

Dialogue involves:

- A free and creative exploration of complex and subtle issues and an assumption that many people have pieces of the answer

- Listening to understand one another—a suspending of one's own view

- Serious conversation in which participants reveal their assumptions and become observers of their own thinking, admitting that others' thinking can improve their own

People generally have the necessary skills for dialogue. Think of times when you engaged in conversation with a colleague to understand what that person thinks and why he or she thinks that way. These are conversations in which each person works hard to grasp the perspective of the other by not being judgmental and instead trying to see the world through the other's eyes.

Dialogue Includes These Expectations

No agreement will necessarily be reached. Dialogue is not a search for agreement on one right answer. It is expected that some of the beliefs people hold sacred will be challenged.

When dialogue occurs, controversy is an unavoidable outcome. When controversy is managed constructively, it promotes an uncertainty about one's own views—which ideally leads to an active search for information, resulting in a reorganization of one's perception or appreciation of a situation and perhaps one's values as applied to the situation. The learning is in the conversation, and the participants' contributions act as stimuli for deeper inquiry. Dialogue embraces divergent thinking and should be approached with no particular result in mind but with the intention of developing deeper understanding and insight that may lead to convergence on a good answer or answers. (Discussion of dialogue adapted from D. Bohm, *On Dialogue* [New York: Routledge, 2004, originally published 1996], and P. Senge, *The Fifth Discipline: The Art and Practice of the Learning Organization* [New York: Random House/Crown. 2006].)

Getting Started with Dialogue

A dialogue can help team members view a problem from each other's perspectives and enhance their creativity.

- Practice *suspension of judgment and reaction*. If someone in your group has a different view or seems to disagree with you, do not react immediately to defend your view. Be aware of what is going on and how your past experience shapes your assumptions about what you are hearing.

- Practice *containment*. Dialogue *contains* conflict rather than suppressing it, avoiding it, or allowing it to become a win-lose battle. To foster this containment, remind yourself of the group's commitment to working together.

- See each other as colleagues. Willingness to consider each other as colleagues does not mean you all need to agree or share the same views. People must want the benefits of dialogue more than they want to hold onto privileges of rank or misplaced certainty.

Suggestions for the Facilitator

- Help everyone speak to the center of the group, and not to each other. Encourage the participants to understand what other speakers mean.

- Encourage the participants to take responsibility for making themselves understood.

Worksheet 43

Ground Rules for Participants

- Speak from personal experience and speak from your own understanding of what is going on (do not invoke an outside authority).

- Ask honest and open questions, ones that you do not know the answers to.

- Do not try to fix, save, or advise anyone or set anyone straight.

- Teach yourself, not others.

- Speak to the center, not to another individual in the group.

Reflective Questions for Participants

- What in my experience has led me to believe things the way I do, and why do I believe this way?

- Do I accurately understand what is being said here?

Worksheet 43

WORKSHEET 44
Identifying Needed Formative Evaluations

Instructions. Formative evaluations are used to improve program or project quality (J. L. Fitzpatrick, J. R. Sanders, and B. R. Worthen, *Program Evaluation: Alternative Approaches and Practical Guidelines*, 3rd ed. (Boston: Pearson Education, 2004, p. 20). The typical audience is program managers and staff. Typically, internal evaluators do the work, but they may rely on help from external evaluators. A key feature of a formative evaluation is the provision of feedback to decision makers and involved personnel in such a way that it can be used to improve the program or project. The process is diagnostic, not judgmental. The focus is on what is working, what is not, what modifications would improve things, and how those changes might be made. Key formative evaluation design questions include the following:

- What information is needed?
- Who needs it?
- What evaluation design will produce the needed information?
- How should the information be collected and analyzed?
- How should recommendations be developed and fed back to those who need them?

1. Which strategies, programs, projects, or operations would benefit from a formative evaluation?

2. For each formative evaluation, what kinds of information would be particularly helpful?

3. Who would benefit from having this information?

4. What are your thoughts about the way this information might be collected in order to be most understandable, valid, reliable, and useful? In other words, what are your thoughts about the best formative evaluation design?

5. How would you ensure that baselines and performance indicators of some sort exist, so that people will have something against which to measure progress?

6. How would you identify strengths and weaknesses and other sorts of comparisons and contrasts in order to facilitate learning?

7. How would you ensure that the process is seen as helpful?

8. Who will conduct the evaluation?

9. Is outside assistance necessary?

WORKSHEET 45

Employee Performance Self-Review

Instructions. Fill out this self-review to reflect on your own performance and to prepare for a meeting with your supervisor.

1. What do you see as your greatest strengths?

2. Do you feel that your job enables you to play to your strengths? If no, please explain.

3. Do you think you met your goals last year? Please list your goals and comment on your successes and/or any frustrations or disappointments.

4. Are there areas in your work life you would like to improve? What can this organization do to help you meet your goals?

5. Do you have comments or suggestions about the functioning of your team or how you would like to be supervised?

6. How do you see your work contributing to the mission and strategic goals of the organization?

Worksheet 45

FY (Ending Year) Goals		
Personal Goals	**Action Taken**	**Results**

FY (Coming Year) Goals		
Personal Goals	**Actions to Be Taken**	**Resources That Are Needed (time, help, and so forth)**

Source: Adapted from materials developed by The Loft Literary Center, Minneapolis, Minnesota.

Worksheet 45

Implementing and Sustaining Your Strategic Plan.

Companion Performance Review to Be Completed by Supervisor

1. What do you see as this employee's greatest strengths?

2. Do you feel that this employee's job enables him or her to play to his or her strengths? If no, please explain.

3. Do you feel that this employee met his or her goals last year? Please list these goals and comment on the employee's successes and on any frustrations or disappointments.

4. Are there areas in this employee's work life you would like to see him or her improve? What can this organization do to help this employee meet his or her goals?

5. Do you and this employee have suggestions for improving the supervision of the employee or the functioning of your team?

6. How will this employee influence this organization's future as guided by the strategic plan?

Source: Adapted from materials developed by The Loft Literary Center, Minneapolis, Minnesota.

WORKSHEET 46

Performance Review and Development Plan Process

Instructions. Performance reviews of individual employees should focus both on performance and professional development. A good review process can be used as a tool to focus on strategic work, keep good people, and help them improve. Consider the following steps and use the worksheet that follows as an example of a potentially useful performance review:

1. Prepare and give to the employee a memo with the date and time of his or her performance review meeting.

2. Review the position description and your documentation and reflections on the employee's performance for the performance review period.

3. Meet with the employee to discuss his or her performance.

4. Present the performance review and your suggested development plan to the employee for his or her review, comments, and signature. Allow the employee reasonable time to study the review and development plan before returning it to you signed.

5. Review the employee's comments, and make revisions and adjustments that seem appropriate and wise.

During the review process fill in the following form and for each competency area check the appropriate box to indicate that the employee needs improvement, meets expectations, or exceeds expectations.

Competency Ratings

1. Communication

   ☐ Needs Improvement   ☐ Meets Expectations   ☐ Exceeds Expectations

   Examples of performance:

2. Customer Service

   ☐ Needs Improvement   ☐ Meets Expectations   ☐ Exceeds Expectations

   Examples of performance:

3. Decision Making and Problem Solving

   ☐ Needs Improvement   ☐ Meets Expectations   ☐ Exceeds Expectations

   Examples of performance:

4. Interpersonal Skills

   ☐ Needs Improvement   ☐ Meets Expectations   ☐ Exceeds Expectations

   Examples of performance:

5. Technical Skills and Knowledge

    ☐ Needs Improvement   ☐ Meets Expectations   ☐ Exceeds Expectations

Examples of performance:

6. Time Management

    ☐ Needs Improvement   ☐ Meets Expectations   ☐ Exceeds Expectations

Examples of performance:

7. People Management

    ☐ Needs Improvement   ☐ Meets Expectations   ☐ Exceeds Expectations

Examples of performance:

Worksheet 46

Implementing and Sustaining Your Strategic Plan.

Major Achievements

Describe the employee's major achievements during the performance review period:

Contributions to the Organization's Strategic Goals

Before proceeding further with the review, list the *organization's* values and strategic goals.

Organization's values:

Organization's strategic goals:

Now, using the employee's current performance goals, evaluate his or her contribution to the achievement of the organization's strategic goals in the period under review.

☐ Needs Improvement   ☐ Meets Expectations   ☐ Exceeds Expectations

Examples of contributions to the organization's strategic goals:

New Performance Goals

Using the employee's job description and considering the organization's values and strategic goals (listed previously), identify 3 to 5 performance goals to be accomplished by the employee in the upcoming performance review and development plan period.

3 to 5 performance goals:

Describe how these performance goals relate to organizational values and strategic goals:

Proposed Employee Development Plan

Identify development goals for the upcoming performance review and development plan period. These goals should enhance the employee's development and serve the needs of the organization.

Development Goal	Activities to Accomplish	Timeline

Source: Adapted from a performance review form used by the Minneapolis Park and Recreation Board, Minneapolis, Minnesota.

Worksheet 46

Implementing and Sustaining Your Strategic Plan.

WORKSHEET 47

Coaching for Successful Implementation

Instructions. Coaching is often important for improving individual and team performance. A coach works one on one with individuals and with groups to draw on their individual strengths and to develop the competencies they will need to be effective during implementation and in the future. Leaders who see themselves as coaches also see their group members as individuals of innate talent and worth.

Keep in mind that coaching is working with others at the edge of their comfort zone. The effective coach provides both challenge and support. Support is essential for change; it is a foundation that allows individuals and groups to take risks. Providing challenge means being willing to push, voice the hard truths, confront constructively, and reject the easy, but wrong, answers.

Coaches play many roles; they

- Help individuals and groups understand the fundamentals, master needed skills, and stay focused on the task.

- Build teamwork so that complementarities are emphasized and coordinated and the group works together in a reasonable and effective way.

- Help people evaluate and adjust; sometimes group members need to be repositioned, strategies need to change, immediate needs must be addressed, and future circumstances anticipated.

- Reinforce good behavior and learning and motivate individuals and groups to perform well; this may mean correcting problems without destroying self-confidence; praising good efforts; and acting as a good role model for others.

Coaching skills include

- Building trust

- Setting expectations

- Listening

- Communicating verbally, including providing feedback, giving recognition, questioning, informing, and instructing

- Mentoring

- Observing and measuring performance, including gathering data, giving praise, and pointing out areas for improvement

- Setting a positive and constructive example

Actual and potential implementation coaches should answer the following questions and use the responses to improve their coaching of individuals and groups involved in implementation efforts.

1. Think about coaches or mentors who have been helpful to you. Describe what was helpful about their approach.

2. Describe your own coaching. What works well? How would you like to improve?

3. What is your personal commitment to the person's or group's development?

4. What does this person or group do well?

5. What are the person's or group's goals in relation to strategic plan implementation?

6. How can personal buy-in for strategy implementation be developed?

7. How can you facilitate congruence between this person's or group's goals and strategic priorities?

8. In light of the goals, how does this person or group need to improve?

WORKSHEET 48

Professional Development Request Form

Instructions. Persons (or I-Teams) wishing to request professional development help should fill out this form and discuss the opportunity with their supervisor or program director.

The request will be discussed and approved or denied.

If it is approved, the recipient should write a brief report after the professional development work is completed and share his or her experience with the rest of the staff.

Name: _____

Department: _____

Supervisor's signature: _____

Today's date: _____

Professional development opportunity:

Sponsoring organization:

Date of opportunity:

Description of opportunity or class:

Estimated cost associated with opportunity:

   Fee:

   Travel:

   Lodging:

   Per diem:

   Other:

   Total:

Please describe how you hope this opportunity will help you meet your work goals *and* help this organization accomplish its strategic goals.

Please list other opportunities (feel free to dream) that you might like in the future.

What kind of in-service training or development do you think would be useful for your work team or the entire staff?

Submit this completed form to your supervisor.

Source: Adapted from materials developed by The Loft Literary Center, Minneapolis, Minnesota.

Step 11

Putting It All Together in Strategy Maps and Action Plans

Purpose of Step

Strategy implementation is often a complicated multiyear process. The purpose of Step 11 is to integrate and summarize the results of the previous steps into clearly understandable, manageable, and actionable form via multiyear strategy maps and yearlong or shorter action plans (often called work plans).

Strategy maps present a big-picture view of what the organization (or collaboration or community), or one or more selected parts of it, is doing to create significant public value overall and where packages of specific actions are needed to implement the strategies. Strategy maps are "*word-and-arrow* diagrams in which ideas and actions are causally linked to one another through the use of arrows. The arrows indicate how one idea or action leads to another" (Bryson, Ackermann, Eden, & Finn, 2004, p. 4). The basic logical form used for strategy maps is displayed in Figure 1 (in the Preface), which outlines how public value is created, in part, via meeting mandates and fulfilling the mission, achieving goals, and implementing strategies consisting of ongoing operations and new portfolios of initiatives. Strategy maps add important details to this basic form so that operations and new initiatives are guided in appropriate directions. Strategy maps build on two very common group process techniques: brainstorming (see Resource A) and the snow card, or affinity diagram, technique (see Resource B). Brainstorming produces lots of ideas in response to specific questions. The snow card technique helps people cluster the ideas according to common themes or subject matter. Strategy mapping takes the next step by helping implementation leaders, managers, and planners to understand how the ideas within and across clusters are linked. The resulting map can help users make sense of and manage complexity.

Different parts of the implementation management structure are likely to be responsible for different parts of a strategy map developed for the organization as a whole. The implementation coordinating committee (ICC) will be responsible for ensuring desirable performance against the mission, mandates, and goals, and for broad oversight of strategy implementation. Specific sponsors will be in charge of specific strategic goals, strategies, or sets of strategies, and related programs and projects. Program managers (who ideally are also sponsors and champions) will focus on specific programs and projects. Project managers (who ideally will be champions) will be responsible for specific projects.

Note that there are two basic kinds of strategy maps. The first is the action-oriented strategy map (AOSM) (Bryson et al., 2004; Bryson, 2011), the kind emphasized here. The second is the balanced scorecard (BSC) strategy map (Kaplan & Norton, 2004; Niven, 2008). BSC strategy maps can be useful, but they tend to rely on fairly rigid categories and the causal linkages (the arrows) are often quite loose, meaning that BSC maps typically show significant leaps in logic.

Action plans typically have a time frame of one year or less. They spell out the details of what is to be done; who is responsible; where the resources will come from; what results are expected, when, and where; how progress will be monitored; and what process will be used to identify and take any needed corrective or adaptive action. Action plans should be developed for the policy board; the ICC (which may be the same as the policy board); portfolio, program, and project managers; and all I-Teams. Ongoing operations should also make use of action plans.

Possible Desired Implementation Outcomes

- Creation of a strategy map that provides a one- or two-page graphic depiction of the organization's multiyear approach to creating public value

- Regularly updated annual (or more frequent) action plans for the policy board, the ICC (which may be the same as the policy board); portfolio, program, and project managers; all I-Teams; and ongoing operations

- Linkage of the strategy maps and action plans to performance monitoring and interactive learning processes

- A process for reporting on and oversight of implementation efforts (through periodic management reports, Web postings, annual reports, and so forth)

- Accountability for results linked with responsible parties

Worksheet Directions

1. Have implementation planners develop an action-oriented strategy map that pulls together information from Steps 5 and 6. Use Exhibit 3, the action-oriented strategy mapping guide, for pointers.

2. Develop an action plan for the policy board and the ICC, using Worksheet 49.

3. Develop action plans for all strategic initiatives (portfolios, programs, and projects; I-Teams; and ongoing operations), using Worksheet 50.

4. Develop actions plans for all activities that are to be phased out (the stop agenda), using Worksheet 51.

5. Consider using project management software for managing and updating action plans, for example, BaseCamp or Microsoft Project. Worksheet 52 shows a blank Microsoft Project template. Exhibit 4 shows what a portion of an implementation action plan looks like when presented using the Microsoft Project format.

6. Search across all the completed copies of Worksheets 50 and 51 and prepare a separate version of Worksheet 53 for each group or individual who has a responsibility for some aspect of implementation. Again, consider using project management software to highlight group and individual responsibility for tasks.

7. Use copies of Worksheet 54 to keep track of the status of each strategy and action and to foster needed interactive learning about what has worked and how to address any challenges encountered.

8. Use Worksheet 55 to develop an implementation communications process and plan.

9. Worksheet 56 will help decision makers and others develop an *elevator speech*, a brief set of comments that succinctly and memorably summarizes what the implementation effort is about, how the work is being done, why it is important, and for whom it matters.

EXHIBIT 3

Action-Oriented Strategy Mapping (AOSM) Guidelines

Action-oriented strategy mapping (AOSM) involves word-and-arrow diagrams in which the ideas are all phrased in action terms (for example, *get*, *buy*, *do*, *create*, *find*, and so forth) and the arrows indicate causal relationships among ideas—meaning the arrows show what can be expected to lead to what, or what has to happen for something else to happen. An example is presented in Figures 12 and 13 (following this exhibit). The example involves a small college in need of a drastic turnaround. Figure 12 presents the college's goals and strategies, and Figure 13 shows details related to its strategy of increasing student enrollment. (The case is presented in full detail in Bryson et al., 2004, pp. 153–181.)

Figure 12 shows that the college's mission at present is simply to "Improve Hope College." This mission is hardly inspiring, but given the state of the college when the mapping took place, it was inspiring enough in that it pointed toward a better future. (Note that the numbers are simply place holders for ideas; they are an address in the computer software used to produce finished maps indicating the order in which ideas were created and have no relation to content.). This higher purpose is supported by nine general goals, which are in rounded rectangles. Five of the goals directly support the improve Hope College mission: "relations with the community are productive and respectful," "our students achieve outstanding results," "our college is well managed," "morale at Hope College is high," and "our teachers are well qualified and their teaching is excellent." The remaining four goals support the mission indirectly, through the direct goals. The goals are to be achieved via nine strategies (in italics). Figure 13 shows how the strategy to "increase student enrollment" is to be pursued. Five of the other eight strategies directly support it. Note that there is a negative relationship between "increase academic standards" and "increase student enrollment"; the negative relationship is indicated by the minus sign next to the arrow. In other words, increasing academic standards is likely to reduce, not increase enrollment. The figure also shows a number of actions that will need to be taken to implement the strategies.

To prepare an AOSM, the process facilitator guides participants in brainstorming solutions to an issue or problem and writing their ideas on large Post-it notes. The notes are then affixed to a flipchart-sheet-covered wall, participants cluster them into groups, and then they work with the clusters to identify how the ideas are linked together in terms of cause-and-effect or influence. Here is an outline of this process (which is described more fully in Bryson et al., 2004; Bryson & Carroll, 2007; and Bryson, 2011).

The basic requirements are

- A group consisting of no more than twelve people; seven people is optimal.

- A facilitator, ideally from outside the group, until the group is able to facilitate itself.

- A large wall.

- Flipchart sheets.

- Masking tape.

- Dark flipchart markers.

- Pencils with erasers.

- Large Post-it notes or half-sheets of 8-1/2 x 11-inch cheap white copy paper.

Follow these steps:

1. Tape the flipchart sheets together on the wall to make a rectangular backdrop for the Post-its. The rectangle should be four to eight sheets wide and two to three sheets high, depending on the size of the group. Flipchart sheets should overlap one another by one inch, so that the entire rectangle can be taken down and moved easily.

2. Draw a horizontal dashed line across the mapping surface one-third of the way down from the top.

3. The facilitator asks each group member to think of solutions or responses to the challenge or issue being considered and to write those ideas on the large Post-it notes, one idea per note, using the markers. For example, if the problem were female illiteracy in a developing country, the facilitator might pose the question, "What should we do to increase female literacy?" *When AOSM is used as part of the implementation process, many answers to the relevant question will already have been articulated in Step 6.* A *starter pack* of Post-its with these previously developed responses should be prepared for the group to use, particularly if these answers have already been adopted by the policy board, are in the strategic plan, or both.

4. The facilitator directs the group members to express their solutions as imperatives: for example, "Have reading materials with female heroes." The idea should be expressed in no more than ten words. When most group members have finished writing, the members place their Post-its on the flipchart-covered wall. (Note that the process as described here assumes that participants can read and write the same language. If participants do not, interpreters may be needed.)

5. The facilitator leads participants in clustering the Post-its according to common themes or subjects, placing the clusters *below* the horizontal dashed line. Within the clusters, the more general, abstract, or goal-oriented ideas are moved toward the top and the more concrete, specific, and detailed ideas toward the bottom. The facilitator asks participants to name each cluster and places a new Post-it with that name above each cluster. These clusters typically represent strategic issue or option areas.

6. The facilitator works with participants to pencil in arrows indicating linkages within and between ideas. An arrow pointing from Post-it A to Post-it B indicates that the action described on Post-it A causes, influences, or precedes the action described on B; conversely the action on Post-it B is an effect, outcome, or follow-up to the action on A. The way to work down a chain of arrows is to keep asking, "How would you do that?" or, "What would it take to do that?" The way to work up a chain of arrows is to keep asking, "What would happen if we did that?" or, "What would the consequences be if we did that?" Once the group agrees on the placement of the arrows, draw them in permanently.

7. The group now has a map of ideas in which specific actions or options are located toward the bottom and (potential) strategies (as bundles of actions) are in the middle. Nothing should appear above the horizontal dashed line yet. The strategies are basically answering the question, *What should we do?* The arrows heading toward the strategies indicate *how* the strategies might be accomplished.

8. The facilitator then encourages the group to think further about what they hope to achieve by carrying out or pursuing the bundles of actions on the map. The responses, or "higher" goals, are written on new Post-its and placed above the horizontal dashed line, in the upper third of the map. Arrows are drawn from previously posted strategies to the goals the strategies will contribute to. Again, a starter pack of any already developed responses should be prepared for the group to use, particularly if these responses have already been adopted by the policy board, are in the strategic plan, or both. Specifically, there should be a fairly direct link from every cluster of actions to one or more adopted goals, mission elements, or mandates. In other words, the responses above the line answer the questions, *Why* should we pursue these strategies? and, What are our goals and mission for these strategies?

9. Finally, through a workshop-type process, the group members should agree on the map's logic (that is, they should be clear that the work-and-arrow links make sense) and on what should be done, how, and why. The group may wish to prioritize the actions, strategies, and goals on the map. The facilitator might give everyone five red dots to place on the five ideas he or she considers most vital. This process can be much more elaborate, but the simple version presented here is typically adequate for compiling an overall strategy map to guide more detailed implementation.

10. The map produced can be preserved as is, translated into an outline, or reproduced using computer graphics. An especially useful version of the map is likely to be a high-level overview that includes just mission, goals, and strategies, as in Figure 12. An overview can help everyone see the organization's big picture regarding aspirations and key strategies for achieving them.

Figure 14 summarizes the logic structure of an AOSM and the questions that are asked to prompt answers at different places in that logic structure.

FIGURE 12

Hope College's Goals and Strategies

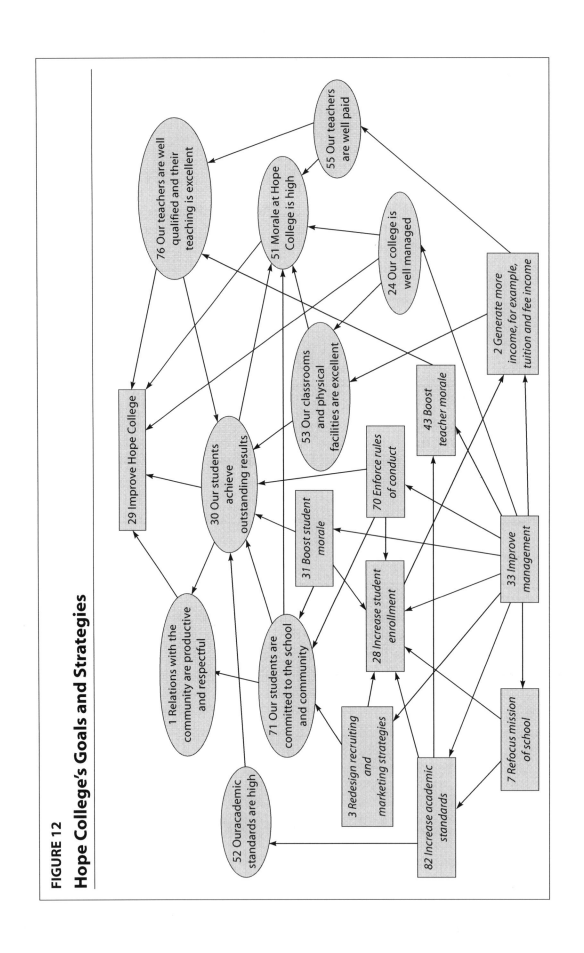

FIGURE 13

Hope College's Strategy for Increasing Student Enrollment

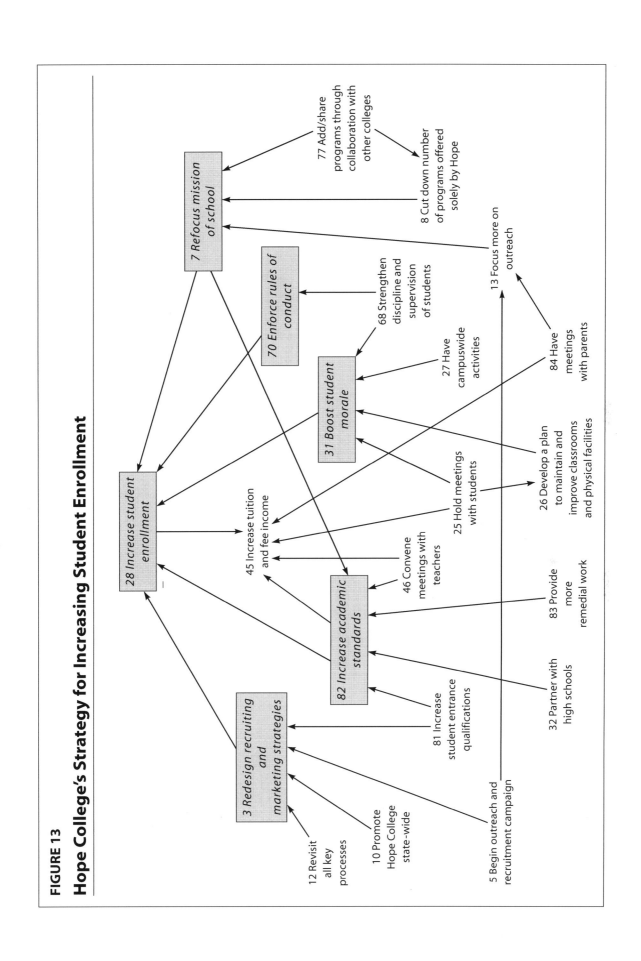

FIGURE 14

Structure of an Action-Oriented Strategy Map

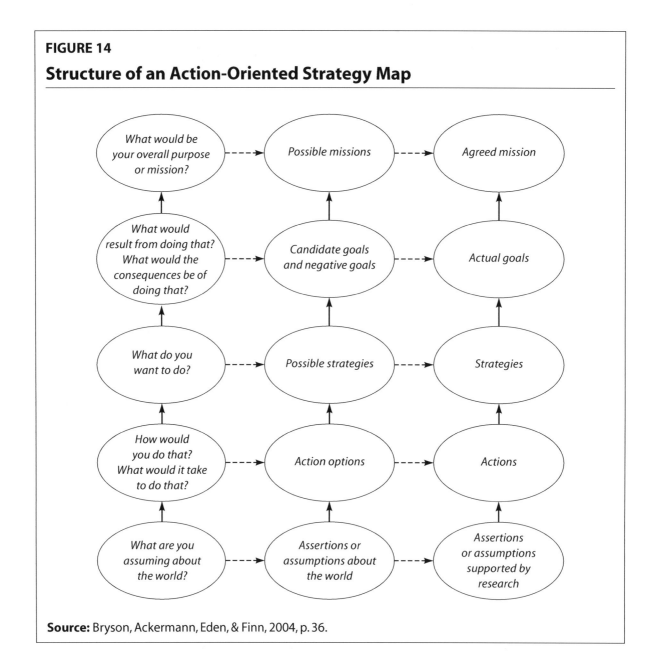

Source: Bryson, Ackermann, Eden, & Finn, 2004, p. 36.

WORKSHEET 49

Board Action Plan

Instructions. Boards have a variety of functions that are important for guiding strategy implementation and preparing the organization for the next round of strategy change. Boards have three basic functions (R. P. Chait, W. P. Ryan, & B. E. Taylor, *Governing as Leadership* [Hoboken, NJ: Wiley, 2004]):

- Framing problems and making sense of ambiguous situations
- Setting strategic goals and priorities and staying on course
- Being stewards of assets now and for the future

The first function is related both to the strategic planning process and to the reassessment process covered by Step 12. The second function is also related to strategic planning and to ensuring that priorities and directions are maintained and adjusted to changing circumstances in desirable ways. The final function is also related to keeping the organization on track and making sure it has the capacity to respond to new challenges.

The board should devote work sessions on a regular basis to keeping its action plan current and to reviewing and monitoring progress. The following worksheet is meant to keep the board focused on its role in looking out for the organization as a whole and on its purposes, strategic directions, and performance. It is not an invitation to engage in micromanagement!

Framing Problems and Making Sense of Ambiguous Situations

Concerns Related to Mission, Mandates, or Strategic Goals	Lead Responsibility on Board	Time Frame	Monitoring and Review Process

Worksheet 49

Implementing and Sustaining Your Strategic Plan.

Setting Strategic Goals and Priorities and Staying on Course

Strategic Goal or Priority	Lead Responsibility on Board for Monitoring Implementation Progress	Time Frame	Monitoring and Review Process

Worksheet 49

Implementing and Sustaining Your Strategic Plan.

Stewarding Assets Now and for the Future

Asset Category	Lead Responsibility on Board for Monitoring Performance	Time Frame	Monitoring and Review Process

Source: Adapted from R. P. Chait, W. P. Ryan, & B. E. Taylor, *Governing as Leadership* (Hoboken, NJ: Wiley, 2004).

Worksheet 49

Implementing and Sustaining Your Strategic Plan.

WORKSHEET 50

Action Planning

Instructions. Review Worksheet 27 and other relevant information, and answer the following questions for each strategic initiative.

---

1. Strategic initiative (for example, program, product, service, or project):

2. Relevant strategy:

3. What specific actions must be taken to implement the strategic initiative during the next year (or other relatively short period of time)?

4. What are the expected results and indicators of success?

5. What are the requirements for success?

6. Who are the responsible parties? What are their roles and responsibilities?

Party	Roles and Responsibilities
Policy board	
Implementation coordinating committee	
Portfolio manager	
Program manager	
Project manager	
Implementation team	
Ongoing operations group	
Partners	

Worksheet 50

7. What is the specific time frame? When and where will the actions be taken?

8. What resources will be required, and where will they be obtained?

9. What communication process will be followed?

10. How will the action plan implementation be reviewed and monitored and accountability ensured?

WORKSHEET 51

Action Planning for the Stop Agenda

Instructions. Answer the following questions for each strategy, program, project, other initiative, or part of ongoing operations that is to be phased out.

1. What is to be phased out?

2. Why is it being phased out?

3. Are parts of this activity being transferred to other parts of the organization or elsewhere?

4. What specific actions must be taken to phase out this activity during the next year?

5. What are the expected results (including resources freed up) and indicators of success?

6. What are the requirements for success?

7. Who are the responsible parties? What are their roles and responsibilities?

Party	Roles and Responsibilities
Policy board	
Implementation coordinating committee	
Portfolio manager	
Program manager	
Project manager	
Implementation team	
Ongoing operations group	
Partners	

Worksheet 51

Implementing and Sustaining Your Strategic Plan.

8. What is the specific time frame? When and where will the actions be taken?

9. What resources will be required, and where will they be obtained?

10. What communication process will be followed?

11. How will the action plan implementation be reviewed and monitored and accountability ensured?

Microsoft Project Schedule Template

ID	Task Name	Duration	Start	Finish	Predecessors	Resource Names	Qtr 4, 2011			Qtr 1, 2012			Qtr 2, 2012		
							Oct	Nov	Dec	Jan	Feb	Mar	Apr	May	Jun
1															
2															
3															
4															
5															
6															
7															
8															
9															
10															
11															
12															
13															
14															
15															
16															
17															
18															

Project: Sample MS Project Template
Date: Tue 07-27-11

Task	Milestone ◆	External Tasks
Split	Summary	External Milestone ◆
Progress	Project Summary	Deadline ⇨

Page 1

Microsoft Project Schedule Template

ID	Task Name	Duration	Start	Finish	Predecessors	Resource Names	Qtr 4, 2011			Qtr 1, 2012			Qtr 2, 2012		
							Oct	Nov	Dec	Jan	Feb	Mar	Apr	May	Jun
19															
20															
21															
22															
23															
24															
25															
26															
27															
28															
29															
30															

Project: Sample MS Project Template
Date: Tue 07-27-11

Task		Milestone	◆	External Tasks	
Split	....	Summary		External Milestone	◆
Progress		Project Summary		Deadline	⇩

Page 2

Worksheet 52

EXHIBIT 4

Microsoft Project Schedule Template

Los Angeles County—Comprehensive Educational Reform in the Juvenile Halls and Camps

ID	Task Name	Start	Finish
1	**Educational Responsibilities**	**Wed 03-04-09**	**Fri 12-31-10**
2	**1. Recruit Director of School Services**	**Wed 03-04-09**	**Wed 06-30-10**
3	a. Conduct 1st round of recruitment	Wed 03-04-09	Fri 09-04-09
4	b. Conduct 2nd round of recruitment	Mon 10-05-09	Fri 03-26-10
5	c. Hire Director of School Services	Mon 03-29-10	Mon 03-29-10
6	d. Orient & coach Director of School Services	Mon 03-29-10	Wed 06-30-10
7	**2. Implement assessment MDTs**	**Mon 07-27-09**	**Fri 03-26-10**
8	a. Pilot camp assessment/case planning	Mon 07-27-09	Fri 10-02-09
9	b. Obtain approval of juvenile bureaus	Mon 10-05-09	Fri 10-16-09
10	c. Present to JC delinquency judges	Tue 10-20-09	Tue 10-20-09
11	d. Complete flowscript/other documentation	Tue 10-20-09	Fri 10-30-09
12	e. Complete training of CAU/CHQ staff	Tue 10-20-09	Fri 10-30-09
13	f. Update County FERPA MOU to support MDTs	Mon 11-02-09	Fri 12-25-09
14	g. Update County HIPPA MOU to support MDTs	Mon 11-02-09	Fri 12-25-09
15	h. Obtain approvals of FERPA/HIPPA MOUs	Mon 01-04-10	Fri 03-26-10
16	**3. Ensure parent role in youth development**	**Mon 06-15-09**	**Fri 12-31-10**
17	a. Produce initial module of parent training	Mon 06-15-09	Fri 09-11-09
18	b. "Field test" initial module of parent training	Mon 09-14-09	Fri 10-09-09
19	c. Prioritize production of remaining modules	Mon 09-14-09	Fri 10-09-09
20	d. Roll out initial module of parent training	Mon 11-02-09	Fri 12-25-09
21	e. Produce Phase II parent training modules	Mon 01-04-10	Wed 06-30-10
22	f. Produce Phase III parent training modules	Thu 07-01-10	Fri 12-31-10
23	**4. Work with judges to determine ed. rights**	**Mon 04-06-09**	**Fri 01-29-10**
24	a. Recruit Junior Women's volunteers	Mon 04-06-09	Fri 06-26-09
25	b. Train Junior Women's volunteers	Mon 06-29-09	Fri 07-31-09
26	c. Review use of Junior Women's volunteers	Mon 01-04-10	Fri 01-29-10
27	**5. Work with judges to ID surrogates**	**Mon 11-02-09**	**Fri 05-28-10**
28	a. Recruit surrogates	Mon 11-02-09	Fri 12-25-09
29	b. Train surrogates	Mon 01-04-10	Fri 02-26-10
30	c. Review use of surrogates	Mon 04-05-10	Fri 05-28-10
31	**6. Train DPOs to advocate for youth**	**Tue 11-03-09**	**Fri 10-01-10**
32	a. Develop training materials	Tue 11-03-09	Thu 12-31-09
33	b. Obtain STC certification	Mon 01-04-10	Fri 01-29-10
34	c. Train camp DPOs	Mon 02-01-10	Wed 06-30-10
35	d. Train juvenile field DPOs	Mon 02-01-10	Wed 06-30-10
36	e. Conduct fidelity assessment of staff	Mon 07-05-10	Fri 10-01-10

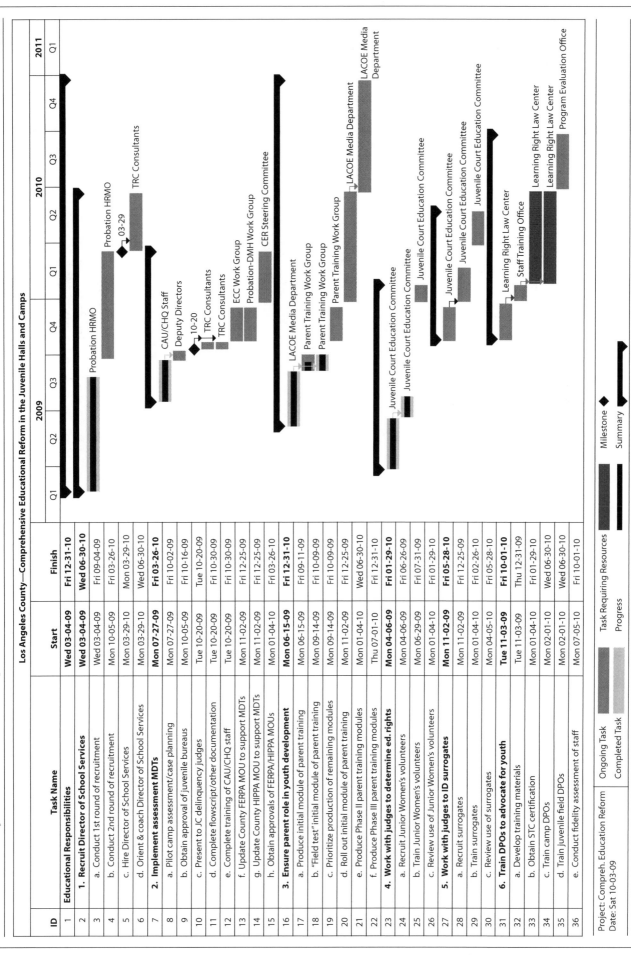

Project: Compreh. Education Reform
Date: Sat 10-03-09

Task Requiring Resources	Ongoing Task
Progress	Completed Task
Milestone ◆	
Summary	

Page 1

EXHIBIT 4
Microsoft Project Schedule Template (Continued)

Los Angeles County—Comprehensive Educational Reform in the Juvenile Halls and Camps

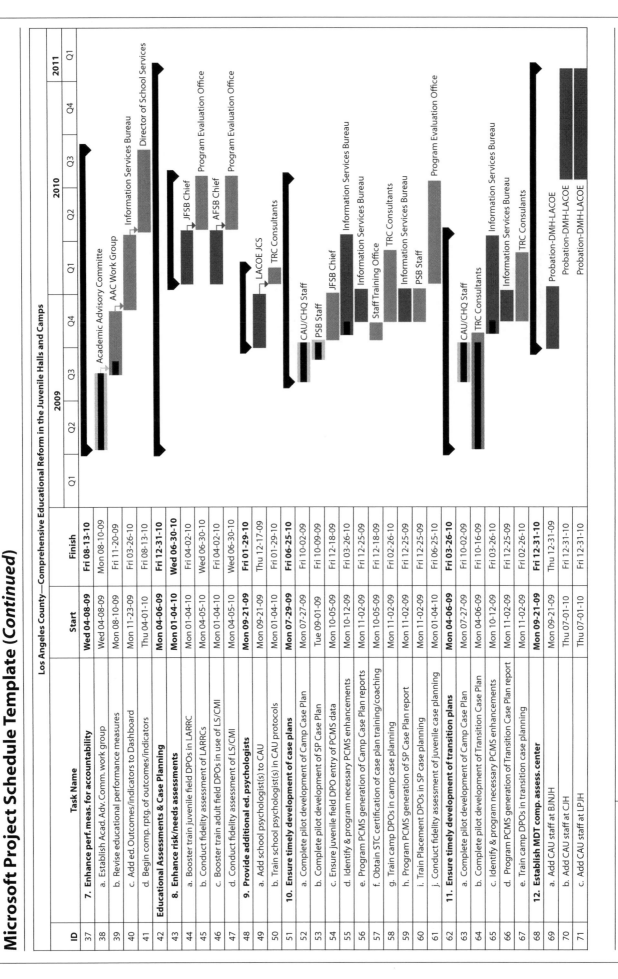

ID	Task Name	Start	Finish
37	**7. Enhance perf. meas. for accountability**	**Wed 04-08-09**	**Fri 08-13-10**
38	a. Establish Acad. Adv. Comm. work group	Wed 04-08-09	Mon 08-10-09
39	b. Revise educational performance measures	Mon 08-10-09	Fri 11-20-09
40	c. Add ed. Outcomes/indicators to Dashboard	Mon 11-23-09	Fri 03-26-10
41	d. Begin comp. rptg. of outcomes/indicators	Thu 04-01-10	Fri 08-13-10
42	**Educational Assessments & Case Planning**	**Mon 04-06-09**	**Fri 12-31-10**
43	**8. Enhance risk/needs assessments**	**Mon 01-04-10**	**Wed 06-30-10**
44	a. Booster train juvenile field DPOs in LARRC	Mon 01-04-10	Fri 04-02-10
45	b. Conduct fidelity assessment of LARRCs	Mon 04-05-10	Wed 06-30-10
46	c. Booster train adult field DPOs in use of LS/CMI	Mon 01-04-10	Fri 04-02-10
47	d. Conduct fidelity assessment of LS/CMI	Mon 04-05-10	Wed 06-30-10
48	**9. Provide additional ed. psychologists**	**Mon 09-21-09**	**Fri 01-29-10**
49	a. Add school psychologist(s) to CAU	Mon 09-21-09	Thu 12-17-09
50	b. Train school psychologists(s) in CAU protocols	Mon 01-04-10	Fri 01-29-10
51	**10. Ensure timely development of case plans**	**Mon 07-29-09**	**Fri 06-25-10**
52	a. Complete pilot development of Camp Case Plan	Mon 07-27-09	Fri 10-02-09
53	b. Complete pilot development of SP Case Plan	Tue 09-01-09	Fri 10-09-09
54	c. Ensure juvenile field DPO entry of PCMS data	Mon 10-05-09	Fri 12-18-09
55	d. Identify & program necessary PCMS enhancements	Mon 10-12-09	Fri 03-26-10
56	e. Program PCMS generation of Camp Case Plan reports	Mon 11-02-09	Fri 12-25-09
57	f. Obtain STC certification of case plan training/coaching	Mon 10-05-09	Fri 12-18-09
58	g. Train camp DPOs in camp case planning	Mon 11-02-09	Fri 02-26-10
59	h. Program PCMS generation of SP Case Plan report	Mon 11-02-09	Fri 12-25-09
60	i. Train Placement DPOs in SP case planning	Mon 11-02-09	Fri 12-25-09
61	j. Conduct fidelity assessment of juvenile case planning	Mon 01-04-10	Fri 06-25-10
62	**11. Ensure timely development of transition plans**	**Mon 04-06-09**	**Fri 03-26-10**
63	a. Complete pilot development of Camp Case Plan	Mon 07-27-09	Fri 10-02-09
64	b. Complete pilot development of Transition Case Plan	Mon 04-06-09	Fri 10-16-09
65	c. Identify & program necessary PCMS enhancements	Mon 10-12-09	Fri 03-26-10
66	d. Program PCMS generation of Transition Case Plan report	Mon 11-02-09	Fri 12-25-09
67	e. Train camp DPOs in transition case planning	Mon 11-02-09	Fri 02-26-10
68	**12. Establish MDT comp. assess. center**	**Mon 09-21-09**	**Fri 12-31-10**
69	a. Add CAU staff at BJNJH	Mon 09-21-09	Thu 12-31-09
70	b. Add CAU staff at CJH	Thu 07-01-10	Fri 12-31-10
71	c. Add CAU staff at LPJH	Thu 07-01-10	Fri 12-31-10

Project: Compreh. Education Reform
Date: Sat 10-03-09

| Task Requiring Resources | Ongoing Task | Milestone |
| Progress | Completed Task | Summary |

Page 2

EXHIBIT 4

Microsoft Project Schedule Template (*Continued*)

Los Angeles County—Comprehensive Educational Reform in the Juvenile Halls and Camps

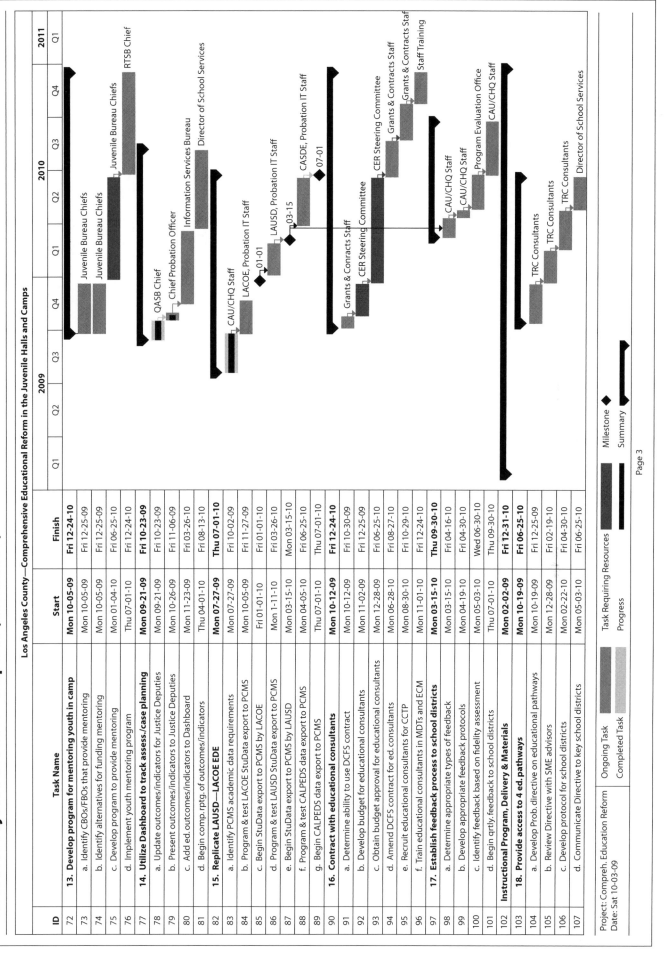

ID	Task Name	Start	Finish
72	**13. Develop program for mentoring youth in camp**	**Mon 10-05-09**	**Fri 12-24-10**
73	a. Identify CBOs/FBOs that provide mentoring	Mon 10-05-09	Fri 12-25-09
74	b. Identify alternatives for funding mentoring	Mon 10-05-09	Fri 12-25-09
75	c. Develop program to provide mentoring	Mon 01-04-10	Fri 06-25-10
76	d. Implement youth mentoring program	Thu 07-01-10	Fri 12-24-10
77	**14. Utilize Dashboard to track assess./case planning**	**Mon 09-21-09**	**Fri 10-23-09**
78	a. Update outcomes/indicators for Justice Deputies	Mon 09-21-09	Fri 10-23-09
79	b. Present outcomes/indicators to Justice Deputies	Mon 10-26-09	Fri 11-06-09
80	c. Add ed. outcomes/indicators to Dashboard	Mon 11-23-09	Fri 03-26-10
81	d. Begin comp. rptg. of outcomes/indicators	Thu 04-01-10	Fri 08-13-10
82	**15. Replicate LAUSD—LACOE EDE**	**Mon 07-27-09**	**Thu 07-01-10**
83	a. Identify PCMS academic data requirements	Mon 07-27-09	Fri 10-02-09
84	b. Program & test LACOE StuData export to PCMS	Mon 10-05-09	Fri 11-27-09
85	c. Begin StuData export to PCMS by LACOE	Fri 01-01-10	Fri 01-01-10
86	d. Program & test LAUSD StuData export to PCMS	Mon 1-11-10	Fri 03-26-10
87	e. Begin StuData export to PCMS by LAUSD	Mon 03-15-10	Mon 03-15-10
88	f. Program & test CALPEDS data export to PCMS	Mon 04-05-10	Fri 06-25-10
89	g. Begin CALPEDS data export to PCMS	Thu 07-01-10	Thu 07-01-10
90	**16. Contract with educational consultants**	**Mon 10-12-09**	**Fri 12-24-10**
91	a. Determine ability to use DCFS contract	Mon 10-12-09	Fri 10-30-09
92	b. Develop budget for educational consultants	Mon 11-02-09	Fri 12-25-09
93	c. Obtain budget approval for educational consultants	Mon 12-28-09	Fri 06-25-10
94	d. Amend DCFS contract for ed. consultants	Mon 06-28-10	Fri 08-27-10
95	e. Recruit educational consultants for CCTP	Mon 08-30-10	Fri 10-29-10
96	f. Train educational consultants in MDTs and ECM	Mon 11-01-10	Fri 12-24-10
97	**17. Establish feedback process to school districts**	**Mon 03-15-10**	**Thu 09-30-10**
98	a. Determine appropriate types of feedback	Mon 03-15-10	Fri 04-16-10
99	b. Develop appropriate feedback protocols	Mon 04-19-10	Fri 04-30-10
100	c. Identify feedback based on fidelity assessment	Mon 05-03-10	Wed 06-30-10
101	d. Begin qrtly. feedback to school districts	Thu 07-01-10	Thu 09-30-10
102	**Instructional Program, Delivery & Materials**	**Mon 02-02-09**	**Fri 12-31-10**
103	**18. Provide access to 4 ed. pathways**	**Mon 10-19-09**	**Fri 06-25-10**
104	a. Develop Prob. directive on educational pathways	Mon 10-19-09	Fri 12-25-09
105	b. Review Directive with SME advisors	Mon 12-28-09	Fri 02-19-10
106	c. Develop protocol for school districts	Mon 02-22-10	Fri 04-30-10
107	d. Communicate Directive to key school districts	Mon 05-03-10	Fri 06-25-10

Project:: Compreh. Education Reform
Date: Sat 10-03-09

Task Requiring Resources | Ongoing Task | Milestone ◆
Progress | Completed Task | Summary

Page 3

EXHIBIT 4

Microsoft Project Schedule Template (*Continued*)

Los Angeles County—Comprehensive Educational Reform in the Juvenile Halls and Camps

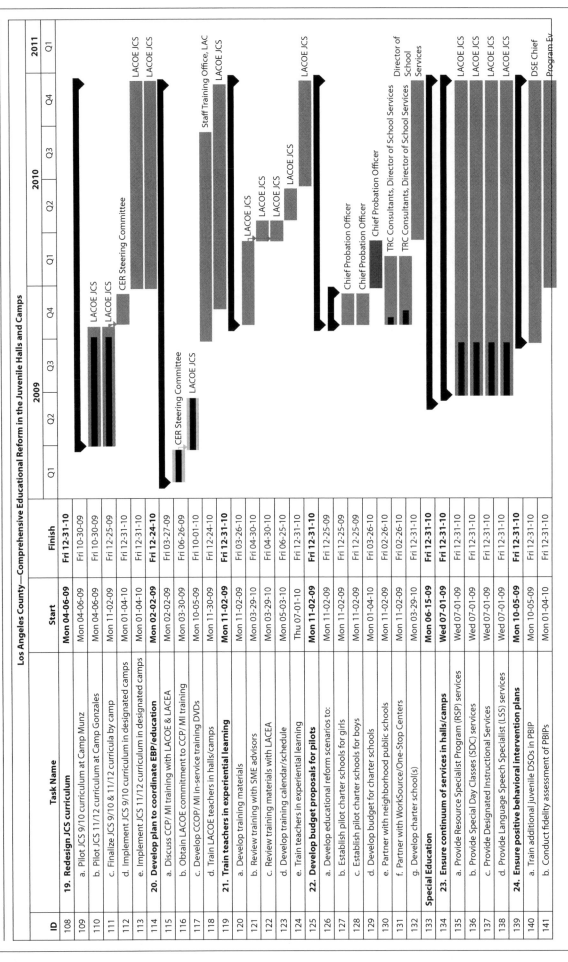

ID	Task Name	Start	Finish
108	**19. Redesign JCS curriculum**	**Mon 04-06-09**	**Fri 12-31-10**
109	a. Pilot JCS 9/10 curriculum at Camp Munz	Mon 04-06-09	Fri 10-30-09
110	b. Pilot JCS 11/12 curriculum at Camp Gonzales	Mon 04-06-09	Fri 10-30-09
111	c. Finalize JCS 9/10 & 11/12 curricula by camp	Mon 11-02-09	Fri 12-25-09
112	d. Implement JCS 9/10 curriculum in designated camps	Mon 01-04-10	Fri 12-31-10
113	e. Implement JCS 11/12 curriculum in designated camps	Mon 01-04-10	Fri 12-31-10
114	**20. Develop plan to coordinate EBP/education**	**Mon 02-02-09**	**Fri 12-24-10**
115	a. Discuss CCP/ MI training with LACOE & LACEA	Mon 02-02-09	Fri 03-27-09
116	b. Obtain LACOE commitment to CCP/ MI training	Mon 03-30-09	Fri 06-26-09
117	c. Develop CCOP/ MI in-service training DVDs	Mon 10-05-09	Fri 10-01-10
118	d. Train LACOE teachers in halls/camps	Mon 11-30-09	Fri 12-24-10
119	**21. Train teachers in experiential learning**	**Mon 11-02-09**	**Fri 12-31-10**
120	a. Develop training materials	Mon 11-02-09	Fri 03-26-10
121	b. Review training with SME advisors	Mon 03-29-10	Fri 04-30-10
122	c. Review training materials with LACEA	Mon 03-29-10	Fri 04-30-10
123	d. Develop training calendar/schedule	Mon 05-03-10	Fri 06-25-10
124	e. Train teachers in experiential learning	Thu 07-01-10	Fri 12-31-10
125	**22. Develop budget proposals for pilots**	**Mon 11-02-09**	**Fri 12-31-10**
126	a. Develop educational reform scenarios to:	Mon 11-02-09	Fri 12-25-09
127	b. Establish pilot charter schools for girls	Mon 11-02-09	Fri 12-25-09
128	c. Establish pilot charter schools for boys	Mon 11-02-09	Fri 12-25-09
129	d. Develop budget for charter schools	Mon 01-04-10	Fri 03-26-10
130	e. Partner with neighborhood public schools	Mon 11-02-09	Fri 02-26-10
131	f. Partner with WorkSource/One-Stop Centers	Mon 11-02-09	Fri 02-26-10
132	g. Develop charter school(s)	Mon 03-29-10	Fri 12-31-10
133	**Special Education**	**Mon 06-15-09**	**Fri 12-31-10**
134	**23. Ensure continuum of services in halls/camps**	**Wed 07-01-09**	**Fri 12-31-10**
135	a. Provide Resource Specialist Program (RSP) services	Wed 07-01-09	Fri 12-31-10
136	b. Provide Special Day Classes (SDC) services	Wed 07-01-09	Fri 12-31-10
137	c. Provide Designated Instructional Services	Wed 07-01-09	Fri 12-31-10
138	d. Provide Language Speech Specialist (LSS) services	Wed 07-01-09	Fri 12-31-10
139	**24. Ensure positive behavioral intervention plans**	**Mon 10-05-09**	**Fri 12-31-10**
140	a. Train additional juvenile DSOs in PBIP	Mon 10-05-09	Fri 12-31-10
141	b. Conduct fidelity assessment of PBIPs	Mon 01-04-10	Fri 12-31-10

Project: Compreh. Education Reform
Date: Sat 10-03-09

Page 4

Legend: Ongoing Task · Completed Task · Task Requiring Resources · Progress · Milestone ◆ · Summary

EXHIBIT 4

Microsoft Project Schedule Template (*Continued*)

Los Angeles County—Comprehensive Educational Reform in the Juvenile Halls and Camps

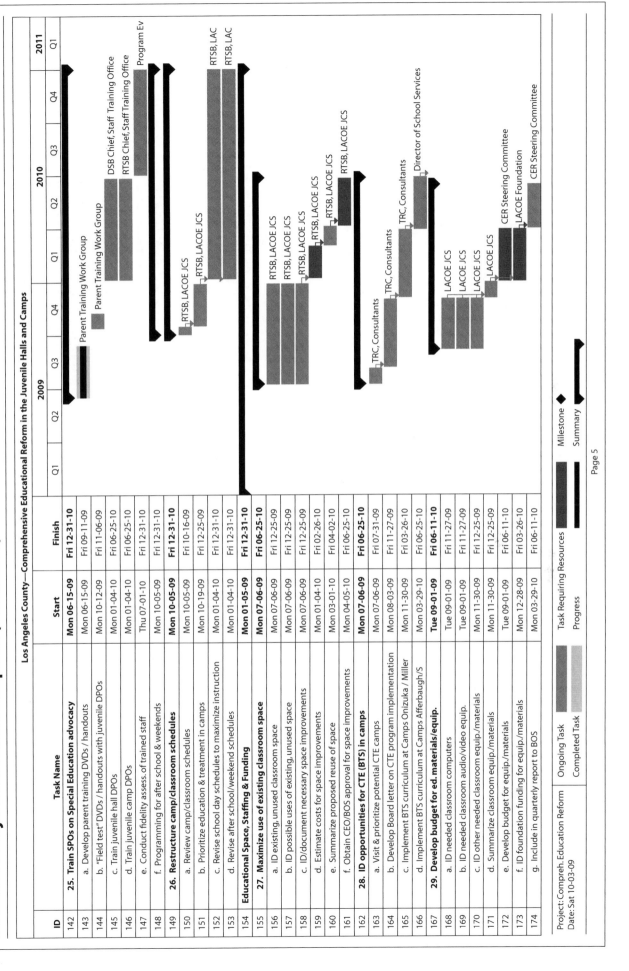

ID	Task Name	Start	Finish
142	**25. Train SPOs on Special Education advocacy**	**Mon 06-15-09**	**Fri 12-31-10**
143	a. Develop parent training DVDs / handouts	Mon 06-15-09	Fri 09-11-09
144	b. "Field test" DVDs / handouts with juvenile DPOs	Mon 10-12-09	Fri 11-06-09
145	c. Train juvenile hall DPOs	Mon 01-04-10	Fri 06-25-10
146	d. Train juvenile camp DPOs	Mon 01-04-10	Fri 06-25-10
147	e. Conduct fidelity assess. of trained staff	Thu 07-01-10	Fri 12-31-10
148	f. Programming for after school & weekends	Mon 10-05-09	Fri 12-31-10
149	**26. Restructure camp/classroom schedules**	**Mon 10-05-09**	**Fri 12-31-10**
150	a. Review camp/classroom schedules	Mon 10-05-09	Fri 10-16-09
151	b. Prioritize education & treatment in camps	Mon 10-19-09	Fri 12-25-09
152	c. Revise school day schedules to maximize instruction	Mon 01-04-10	Fri 12-31-10
153	d. Revise after school/weekend schedules	Mon 01-04-10	Fri 12-31-10
154	**Educational Space, Staffing & Funding**	**Mon 01-05-09**	**Fri 12-31-10**
155	**27. Maximize use of existing classroom space**	**Mon 07-06-09**	**Fri 06-25-10**
156	a. ID existing, unused classroom space	Mon 07-06-09	Fri 12-25-09
157	b. ID possible uses of existing, unused space	Mon 07-06-09	Fri 12-25-09
158	c. ID/document necessary space improvements	Mon 07-06-09	Fri 12-25-09
159	d. Estimate costs for space improvements	Mon 01-04-10	Fri 02-26-10
160	e. Summarize proposed reuse of space	Mon 03-01-10	Fri 04-02-10
161	f. Obtain CEO/BOS approval for space improvements	Mon 04-05-10	Fri 06-25-10
162	**28. ID opportunities for CTE (BTS) in camps**	**Mon 07-06-09**	**Fri 06-25-10**
163	a. Visit & prioritize potential CTE camps	Mon 07-06-09	Fri 07-31-09
164	b. Develop Board letter on CTE program implementation	Mon 08-03-09	Fri 11-27-09
165	c. Implement BTS curriculum at Camps Onizuka / Miller	Mon 11-30-09	Fri 03-26-10
166	d. Implement BTS curriculum at Camps Afferbaugh/S	Mon 03-29-10	Fri 06-25-10
167	**29. Develop budget for ed. materials/equip.**	**Tue 09-01-09**	**Fri 06-11-10**
168	a. ID needed classroom computers	Tue 09-01-09	Fri 11-27-09
169	b. ID needed classroom audio/video equip.	Tue 09-01-09	Fri 11-27-09
170	c. ID other needed classroom equip./materials	Mon 11-30-09	Fri 12-25-09
171	d. Summarize classroom equip./materials	Mon 11-30-09	Fri 12-25-09
172	e. Develop budget for equip./materials	Tue 09-01-09	Fri 06-11-10
173	f. ID foundation funding for equip./materials	Mon 12-28-09	Fri 03-26-10
174	g. Include in quarterly report to BOS	Mon 03-29-10	Fri 06-11-10

Project: Compreh. Education Reform
Date: Sat 10-03-09

Ongoing Task
Completed Task

Task Requiring Resources
Progress

Milestone ◆
Summary

Page 5

EXHIBIT 4

Microsoft Project Schedule Template (*Continued*)

Los Angeles County—Comprehensive Educational Reform in the Juvenile Halls and Camps

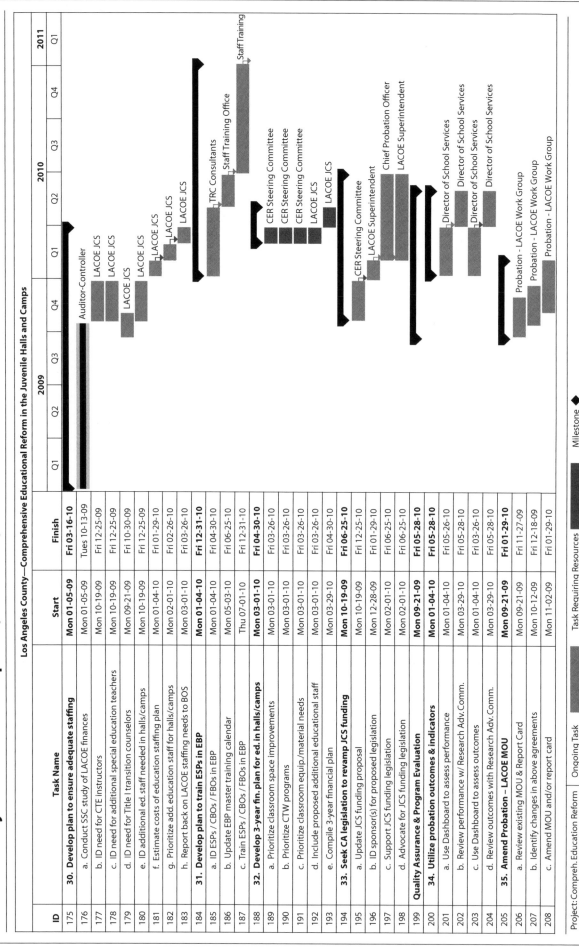

ID	Task Name	Start	Finish
175	**30. Develop plan to ensure adequate staffing**	**Mon 01-05-09**	**Fri 03-16-10**
176	a. Conduct SSC study of LACOE finances	Mon 01-05-09	Tues 10-13-09
177	b. ID need for CTE instructors	Mon 10-19-09	Fri 12-25-09
178	c. ID need for additional special education teachers	Mon 10-19-09	Fri 12-25-09
179	d. ID need for Title I transition counselors	Mon 09-21-09	Fri 10-30-09
180	e. ID additional ed. staff needed in halls/camps	Mon 10-19-09	Fri 12-25-09
181	f. Estimate costs of education staffing plan	Mon 01-04-10	Fri 01-29-10
182	g. Prioritize add. education staff for halls/camps	Mon 02-01-10	Fri 02-26-10
183	h. Report back on LACOE staffing needs to BOS	Mon 03-01-10	Fri 03-26-10
184	**31. Develop plan to train ESPs in EBP**	**Mon 01-04-10**	**Fri 12-31-10**
185	a. ID ESPs / CBOs / FBOs in EBP	Mon 01-04-10	Fri 04-30-10
186	b. Update EBP master training calendar	Mon 05-03-10	Fri 06-25-10
187	c. Train ESPs / CBOs / FBOs in EBP	Thu 07-01-10	Fri 12-31-10
188	**32. Develop 3-year fin. plan for ed. in halls/camps**	**Mon 03-01-10**	**Fri 04-30-10**
189	a. Prioritize classroom space improvements	Mon 03-01-10	Fri 03-26-10
190	b. Prioritize CTW programs	Mon 03-01-10	Fri 03-26-10
191	c. Prioritize classroom equip./material needs	Mon 03-01-10	Fri 03-26-10
192	d. Include proposed additional educational staff	Mon 03-01-10	Fri 03-26-10
193	e. Compile 3-year financial plan	Mon 03-29-10	Fri 04-30-10
194	**33. Seek CA legislation to revamp JCS funding**	**Mon 10-19-09**	**Fri 06-25-10**
195	a. Update JCS funding proposal	Mon 10-19-09	Fri 12-25-09
196	b. ID sponsor(s) for proposed legislation	Mon 12-28-09	Fri 01-29-10
197	c. Support JCS funding legislation	Mon 02-01-10	Fri 06-25-10
198	d. Advocate for JCS funding legislation	Mon 02-01-10	Fri 06-25-10
199	**Quality Assurance & Program Evaluation**	**Mon 09-21-09**	**Fri 05-28-10**
200	**34. Utilize probation outcomes & indicators**	**Mon 01-04-10**	**Fri 05-28-10**
201	a. Use Dashboard to assess performance	Mon 01-04-10	Fri 05-26-10
202	b. Review performance w/ Research Adv. Comm.	Mon 03-29-10	Fri 05-28-10
203	c. Use Dashboard to assess outcomes	Mon 01-04-10	Fri 03-26-10
204	d. Review outcomes with Research Adv. Comm.	Mon 03-29-10	Fri 05-28-10
205	**35. Amend Probation – LACOE MOU**	**Mon 09-21-09**	**Fri 01-29-10**
206	a. Review existing MOU & Report Card	Mon 09-21-09	Fri 11-27-09
207	b. Identify changes in above agreements	Mon 10-12-09	Fri 12-18-09
208	c. Amend MOU and/or report card	Mon 11-02-09	Fri 01-29-10

Project: Compreh. Education Reform
Date: Sat 10-03-09

Task Requiring Resources | Ongoing Task | Milestone ◆

Progress | Completed Task | Summary

Page 6

WORKSHEET 53

Summary of Actions and Responsibilities

Instructions. Use this worksheet to pull together in one place each group's or individual's responsibilities for implementation. Start by reviewing each of the action plans that were prepared using Worksheets 50 and 51. Prepare a separate version of Worksheet 53 for each group or individual who has a responsibility for some aspect of implementation, and include that group's or individual's responsibilities on the worksheet.

This worksheet is for

☐ Policy board

☐ Implementation coordinating committee

☐ Portfolio manager _____

☐ Program manager _____

☐ Project manager _____

☐ Implementation team _____

☐ Ongoing operations group _____

☐ Partner _____

☐ Volunteer _____

☐ Other _____

Action	Responsible Party or Parties	Time Frame from Start to Finish	Monitoring, Review, and Accountability Process

WORKSHEET 54

Strategy/Action Status Report Form

Strategy/Action	Action No.	Scheduled Start/Complete Dates	Task Leader

Task status as of _____

Completed: _____ Date completed: _____ Deliverable _____

Under way: _____ Start date: _____ % Complete: _____

Anticipated completed date: _____

Comments:

1. What has gone well?

2. What challenges or difficulties are being encountered?

3. What might be done to overcome the difficulties or challenges?

4. What other strategies or actions might be needed?

5. What other strategies or actions are these linked to?

Source: Adapted from materials developed by David Schwartz and Farnum Alston of The Resources Company.

Implementation Communications Plan

Instructions. Effective implementation depends on effective communications. Indeed, the message from successful practice is basically, "Communicate, communicate, communicate!" Step 10 attended to the nature and facilitation of dialogue and deliberation in relatively small groups. Here we are more focused on helping implementers think about how communication should occur up, down, and across the organization and with the outside. Use this worksheet to identify the process and schedule for reporting on the implementation components, identifying who is responsible and what the medium is.

Implementation Component	Who Is Responsible for Reporting?	Schedule for Reporting (for example, weekly, monthly, quarterly, yearly, on an as-needed basis)	Audience (for example, manager, ICC, board, funders, external partners, general public)	Process for Reporting (for example, data collection, data presentation, summaries and recommenda-tions, requests for assistance)	Key Performance Indicators to Be Addressed	Medium (for example, face-to-face meeting, e-mail, Web posting, hard-copy report, annual report)
Ongoing operations						
Projects						
Programs						

Component	Who	Schedule	Audience	Reporting	Indicators	Medium
Portfolios						
Specific strategies						
Strategic goal achievement						
Mission fulfillment						
Meeting of mandates						
Other						
Other						

Comments:

WORKSHEET 56

Creating an Elevator Speech

Instructions. An important communication tool is the short speech that provides a compelling message about what the implementation effort is about, how the work is being done, why it is important, and for whom. The message is similar to a vision of success (see Worksheet 22), but is capable of being delivered in sixty seconds—all the time you might have to spend with another person.

Answer the following questions and then ask someone with a flair for simple, direct, vivid language to prepare the elevator speech, perhaps in bullet point form. Different formats might be used to get the message across to different audiences in a variety of ways (such as a brochure, PowerPoint presentation, or the organization's Web site or Facebook page).

1. What is being done? What is being implemented?

2. Who will be helped by this effort? And where are they?

3. How will they be helped?

4. Why is this important for those being helped and for the organization?

5. When is the work being done and when are significant results expected?

6. The sixty-second elevator speech should include the following points:

Part 5

Maintaining, Readjusting, or Terminating Strategies

5
**Maintaining,
Readjusting,
or Terminating
Strategies**

Step 12: Staying the course — or changing it

Step 12

Staying the Course—Or Changing It

Purpose of Step

The purpose of this final step in the Implementation Cycle is to review implemented strategies, the implementation process, and the strategic planning process as a prelude to a new cycle of strategic planning. Much of the work of this phase may have occurred as part of the ongoing Implementation Cycle. However, if an organization has not engaged in an overall review of implemented strategies, the implementation process, and strategic planning for some time, it is useful to mark off this step as a separate one. (This step is the same as Step 10 of the Strategy Change Cycle; see Figure 4.)

In Step 12 you need to reassess strategies—and the strategic issues that prompted them—in order to decide what should be done about them. Strategies may need to be maintained, superseded by other strategies, or terminated for one reason or another. In addition, it is also very useful to review the implementation process to see what has worked, what hasn't, and what might be done to improve it. This exercise involves an important kind of intellectual capacity building and articulation of key lessons that will help to ensure success in future strategic planning and implementation efforts. Finally, an attempt is also made in this step to figure out whether a new round of strategic planning is warranted and, if so, what kind of strategic planning process and when. In doing this review, figure out how to build on the success you have had in implementation and the lessons learned. Strategic planning should build on past efforts. As organizational capacity for strategic thinking, acting, and learning increases, the strategic planning process should become easier.

Possible Desired Planning Outcomes

- Assurance that implemented strategies remain responsive to real needs and problems—and if they don't, consideration of what should be done with them.

- Completion of any necessary or desirable *summative evaluations* of strategy, program, or project processes and impacts to determine the overall worth of a strategy, strategic initiative, program, or project (Fitzpatrick, Sanders, & Worthen, 2004; Patton, 2008), and a determination of what should be done about the strategy, initiative, program, or project.

- Resolution of residual problems that become evident during sustained implementation.

- Clarifications of the strengths, weaknesses, and modifications that would improve the implementation process.

- Clarification of the strengths and weaknesses of the most recent strategic planning effort, and discussion of modifications that might be made in the next round of strategic planning. There should be a natural transition from planning to implementation to evaluation and reassessment to the next round of strategic planning.

- Development of the energy, will, and ideas necessary to revise existing strategies, address important unresolved strategic issues, undertake a full-blown strategic planning exercise, and in general build capacity for organizational responsiveness and capacity for the future.

Worksheet Directions

1. At some point after implementation of the strategic plan has begun, evaluate not only the plan but the overall implementation process and the strategic planning process itself.

2. Strategy implementation is an ongoing process, not a one-time event, and the most effective way to improve it is to evaluate the success of implementation efforts, assessing what has worked, what has not, and what modifications would improve these efforts. Consider who should be involved in this evaluation effort (for example, the ICC, key internal and external stakeholders, outside experts, I-Teams) (Bryson, Patton, & Bowman, 2010).

3. Use Worksheet 57 to evaluate each strategy.

4. Use Worksheet 58 to determine which summative evaluations are needed and to sketch out important elements of the summative evaluation design and process.

5. Use Worksheet 59 to evaluate the implementation process.

6. On the basis of these evaluations and their findings, decide whether a new round of strategic planning is needed and what changes to the process might be indicated. If a new round is thought necessary, fill out Worksheet 60 as a first step in charting possible improvements.

Improving Existing Strategies

Instructions. In deciding what to improve and why, it is important to be clear about the reason why changes are necessary. Is it because of a design flaw in the strategy, unintended consequences, a change in leadership, the organizational design, or the environment, or some other cause?

Strategy	Strengths	Weaknesses	Modifications That Would Improve	Summary Evaluation
				☐ Maintain ☐ Replace with a new or revised element ☐ Terminate
				☐ Maintain ☐ Replace with a new or revised element ☐ Terminate
				☐ Maintain ☐ Replace with a new or revised element ☐ Terminate
				☐ Maintain ☐ Replace with a new or revised element ☐ Terminate

WORKSHEET 58

Identifying Needed Summative Evaluations

Instructions. Summative evaluations are used to determine the overall worth or quality of a strategy, program, or project (or other initiative) for purposes of making a decision about its future (Fitzpatrick, Sanders, & Worthen, 2004, p. 20). The typical audience is administrators, policymakers, funders, or potential adopters. Typically, external evaluators do the work, but they may rely on help from internal evaluators. A key feature of a summative evaluation is the provision of information to decision makers that will allow them to determine whether to continue, modify, or terminate the strategy, program, or project (or perhaps adopt a new strategy). The process is judgmental. Key summative evaluation design questions include

- What results occurred?
- For whom did the results in terms of process and outcomes occur?
- What were the conditions surrounding the strategy, program, or project?
- What did the strategy, program, or project cost?
- How should the information be collected and analyzed?

---

1. Which strategies, programs, projects, or operations would benefit from a summative evaluation?

2. For each summative evaluation, what kinds of judgments would be particularly helpful?

3. Who would benefit from having this information?

4. What are your thoughts about how the way this information might be collected in order to be most understandable, valid, reliable, and useful? In other words, what are your thoughts about the best summative evaluation design?

5. How would you ensure that baselines and performance indicators of some sort exist, so that people will have something against which to measure progress?

6. How would you identify strengths and weaknesses and other sorts of comparisons and contrasts in order to make reasonable judgments?

Worksheet 58

7. How would you ensure that the process serves its intended purpose?

8. Who will conduct the evaluation?

9. Is additional outside or inside assistance necessary?

WORKSHEET 59

Improving the Implementation Process

Instructions. In deciding what to improve and why, it is important to be clear about the reason why changes are necessary. Is it because of a design flaw in the implementation process, unintended consequences, a change in leadership, or the organizational environment, or some other cause?

Implementation Process Category	Implementation Process Element	Strengths	Weaknesses	Modifications That Would Improve	Key Lessons Learned	Summary Evaluation
Understanding implementation and assessing readiness	Step 1: Understanding implementation and assessing readiness					☐ Maintain ☐ Replace with a new or revised element
Getting organized	Step 2: Leading implementation					☐ Maintain ☐ Replace with a new or revised element
	Step 3: Understanding how and why the strategic plan came to be					☐ Maintain ☐ Replace with a new or revised element
	Step 4: Clarifying who the implementation stakeholders are					☐ Maintain ☐ Replace with a new or revised element

Implementing and Sustaining Your Strategic Plan. Copyright © 2011 by John Wiley & Sons, Inc. All rights reserved.

273

Clarifying strategic and operational directions	Step 5: Articulating what the organization's mandates, mission, vision, and values mean for implementation and alignment			☐ Maintain ☐ Replace with a new or revised element
	Step 6: Getting clear about strategies that will continue, will be started, or will be phased out			☐ Maintain ☐ Replace with a new or revised element
Resourcing and structuring implementation, alignment, and ongoing learning	Step 7: Budgeting the work			☐ Maintain ☐ Replace with a new or revised element
	Step 8: Creating an implementation management structure			☐ Maintain ☐ Replace with a new or revised element

Worksheet 59

					☐ Maintain ☐ Replace with a new or revised element
	Step 9: Developing effective implementation teams				☐ Maintain ☐ Replace with a new or revised element
	Step 10: Organizing alignment and learning processes				☐ Maintain ☐ Replace with a new or revised element
	Step 11: Putting it all together in strategy maps and action plans				☐ Maintain ☐ Replace with a new or revised element
Maintaining, readjusting, or terminating strategies	Step 12: Staying the course—or changing it				☐ Maintain ☐ Replace with a new or revised element

Additional comments:

Worksheet 59

Implementing and Sustaining Your Strategic Plan. Copyright © 2011 by John Wiley & Sons, Inc. All rights reserved.

WORKSHEET 60

Improving the Strategic Planning Process

Instructions. In deciding what to improve and why, it is important to be clear about the reason why changes are necessary. Is it because of a design flaw in the strategic planning process, unintended consequences, a change in leadership, the organizational design, or the environment, or some other reason?

Planning Process Element	Strengths	Weaknesses	Modifications That Would Improve	Key Lessons Learned	Summary Evaluation
Initiating and agreeing on a strategic planning process					☐ Maintain ☐ Replace with a new or revised element
Clarifying organizational mandates and mission					☐ Maintain ☐ Replace with a new or revised element
Assessing the environment to identify strengths, weaknesses, opportunities, and challenges (threats)					☐ Maintain ☐ Replace with a new or revised element

				Maintain □ Replace with a new or revised element
Identifying strategic issues				□ Maintain □ Replace with a new or revised element
Formulating strategies and plans to manage the issues				□ Maintain □ Replace with a new or revised element
Strategic plan review and adoption				□ Maintain □ Replace with a new or revised element
Establishing an organizational vision of success				□ Maintain □ Replace with a new or revised element

Worksheet 60

Implementing and Sustaining Your Strategic Plan.

Planning Process Element	Strengths	Weaknesses	Modifications That Would Improve	Key Lessons Learned	Summary Evaluation
Implementing strategies and plans					☐ Maintain ☐ Replace with a new or revised element
Reassessing and revising strategies and plans					☐ Maintain ☐ Replace with a new or revised element

Additional comments:

Worksheet 60

Implementing and Sustaining Your Strategic Plan.

Resources

Brainstorming Guidelines

Brainstorming is a way of producing a large quantity of ideas so that the likelihood of coming up with at least one *high-quality* idea is increased. As Nobel laureate Linus Pauling once said, "The best way to have a good idea is to have a lot of ideas." Guidelines for brainstorming are as follows:

1. Agree to participate in a brainstorming exercise.

2. Appoint a facilitator and a note taker.

3. Focus on a *single* problem or issue. Don't skip around to various problems or try to brainstorm answers to a complex, multiple-factor problem.

4. Have people record their responses to the problem or issue silently and individually on a sheet of scratch paper.

5. Go around the room in round-robin fashion. In each round each individual should offer, in turn, one idea in response to the problem or issue. The recorder should record all ideas in the speaker's own words.

6. Do not criticize or evaluate any of the ideas put forward; they are simply placed before the group and recorded.

7. Be open to hearing some wild ideas in the spontaneity that evolves when the group suspends judgment. Practical considerations are not important at this point. The session is meant to be freewheeling.

8. Emphasize that the quantity of ideas counts, not their quality. All ideas should be expressed, and none should be screened out by any participant. A great number of ideas will increase the likelihood of the group's discovering good ones.

9. Build on the ideas of other group members when possible. Pool people's creativity. Everyone should be free to build onto any idea and to make interesting amalgams from the various suggestions.

10. Foster a congenial, relaxed, cooperative atmosphere.

11. Make sure that all members, no matter how shy and reluctant to contribute, get their ideas heard.

12. Record *all* ideas.

Snow Card Guidelines

The snow card (or affinity diagram) process starts with brainstorming and then goes beyond it by having participants organize the brainstormed ideas into clusters that share a common theme or subject matter. Guidelines for engaging in the snow card process are as follows:

1. Bring a single problem or issue into the group.

2. Have individuals in the group brainstorm as many ideas as possible and record them on individual worksheets.

3. Ask individuals to pick out their five "best items" and to transcribe each one onto its own *snow card*—half of an 8-1/2 by 11 inch sheet of paper, a 5 by 7 inch card, or a large Post-it note.

4. Shuffle the cards; then tape them to a wall in categories. The group should determine the categories after reviewing several of the items. The resulting clusters of cards may resemble a "blizzard" of ideas—hence the term *snow cards*.

5. Establish subcategories as needed.

6. Once all items are on the wall and included in a category, rearrange and tinker with the categories until they make the most sense.

7. Create a label for each category and subcategory on a separate snow card.

8. When finished, take down the cards in their categories and have all the ideas typed up and distributed to the group.

Source: *Based on a technique developed by Richard B. Duke of the University of Michigan and by the Institute of Cultural Affairs (Spencer, 1996).*

Glossary

action plan   A plan for the day-to-day operation of an organization or an organizational unit over the next one to twelve months. It includes a prioritized list of proposed projects as well as plans for all projects that have been funded. Development of an action plan should never require more than two months. The action plan should be reviewed and updated weekly.

alignment   (1) The arrangement of things in a line, meaning in the organizational context that there should be a direct connection all the way from mission to operations on the ground and the production of desired outputs and outcomes. (2) The arrangement and adjustment of things so they are in a proper relationship to each other and therefore better coordination occurs. (3) Essential agreement among individuals, groups, and organizations involved in implementation about what should be done, how, and why.

arenas   Where legislative, executive, or administrative decisions are made and implemented. Examples are legislatures, city councils, boards of directors, cabinets, executive committees, and cartels.

champions   People having primary responsibility for managing implementation efforts on a day-to-day basis.

competencies   Abilities, sets of actions, or strategies at which the organization is particularly good that can be used to perform well against its critical success factors. A competency is the ability to do something well. Having good facilities or a stable budget are not themselves competencies, they are assets; what you are able to do with them might count as competencies. A *core competency* is a competency that is really central to the success of the organization. A *distinctive competency* is a competency that is difficult for others to replicate and so it is a source of enduring organizational advantage. A *distinctive core competency* is not only central to the success of the organization but also helps the organization add more public value and alternative providers. Examples of distinctive core competencies might include ways of delivering services that are unique and especially valued by recipients and ways of maintaining the organization's reputation and people's trust in the organization far in excess of what rivals can do. An *asset* is a resource that may be used to support a competency, distinctive competency, core competency, or distinctive core competency. A *distinctive asset* is a supportive resource that is unique to the organization. A *core distinctive asset* is a distinctive asset that is central to the achievement of the organization's business aspirations.

courts   Where decisions and conduct are judged or evaluated, usually to manage residual conflicts or settle residual disputes. Leaders must be able to invoke the sanctions of formal and informal courts to enforce and reinforce ethical principles, laws, and norms. Some examples are the "court of public opinion" (probably the most powerful court), formal courts or tribunals, professional licensing bodies, and administrators settling disputes among subordinates.

critical success factor   Something that the organization must do or a criterion it must meet in order to be successful in the eyes of its key stakeholders, especially those in its external environment.

decision making   The process of making an authoritative choice about what to do in a particular circumstance.

deliberation   Deliberation denotes careful, intentional, and typically slow consideration of possible choices prior to choosing next steps. Both analysis and synthesis are typically involved, as is dialogue.

dialogue   Dialogue focuses on discovery and listening to each other. The purpose is to increase understanding by hearing what others think and why they think that way. This curiosity to discover each other's assumptions, judgments, values, attitudes, opinions, hopes, expectations, and fears helps everyone learn and creates new, shared understanding.

formative evaluation   An evaluation focused on program or project improvement, not on making summary judgments about effectiveness. Formative evaluation seeks to understand what is going on in a program or project, to analyze what is working and what is not, and to feed information and recommendations back to implementers about how to improve it.

forums   Where people frame and reframe public issues. Formal and informal forums link speakers and audiences to create and communicate shared meaning through discussion, debate, dialogue, and deliberation. Examples are task forces; discussion groups; brainstorming sessions; public hearings; formal debates; discussion and debate via newspapers, television, and radio offerings; plays; conferences; and professional journals.

implementation   The effort to realize in practice an organization's mission, goals, and strategies; the meeting of its mandates; continued organizational learning; and the ongoing creation of public value.

implementation coordinating committee (ICC)   A group, typically composed of sponsors and champions, formed to oversee an overall implementation effort. Individual members may have substantial decision-making authority in their particular areas. The group as a whole usually has some collective decision-making authority or at least substantial influence over decisions. Sometimes policy boards act as ICCs.

implementation management structure Organizational structures and processes designed to help—rather than hinder—strategy implementation and goal achievement. The strategies to be implemented and structures and processes used to manage implementation should be in reasonable alignment.

implementation team (I-Team) A group of people assembled to produce recommendations or to take actions designed to facilitate accomplishment of specified implementation purposes or goals.

leadership The inspiration and mobilization of others to undertake collective action in pursuit of the common good.

logic model A design for the way in which a project, a program, or a policy will process inputs into desired outputs and outcomes, that is, results.

mandate Something an organization is required to do (or not do), often imposed by an external actor. Mandates may be formal, such as laws, rules, or regulations, or informal, such as political mandates for change or deeply held public expectations. Mandates vary in what they require. Sometimes they require that a particular process or set of activities be followed; at other times they specify that a particular standard or outcome be achieved. Sometimes they simply authorize action in a specific area for very general purposes.

mission The organization's purpose—its reason for existence. A *mission statement* should be action oriented and articulate *what* the organization is here to do, and *why*. The statement should also say in general *how* the organization will pursue its work in order to create lasting and significant public value.

ongoing operations Permanent endeavors that produce repetitive outputs, with resources assigned to the repeated accomplishment of basically the same sets of tasks, according to the standards institutionalized in a product or service life cycle.

outcomes The end results, consequences, and ideally benefits of outputs for stakeholders, and the larger meanings attached to those outputs.

outputs The actual things or final products produced by actions, behaviors, programs, projects, products, or services; the direct consequences produced by the implemented strategy, program, project, or other implementation element.

performance measure A means of reasonably objectively assessing the results of programs, products, projects, or services.

portfolio A collection of projects or programs grouped together with other work both to facilitate effective management of that work and to help achieve strategic objectives.

program An ongoing grouping of related projects and operations, managed in a coordinated way to obtain benefits and control not available from managing them individually.

project A temporary endeavor undertaken to produce a specific product, service, or other result.

public value   The public and nonprofit sector equivalent of *shareholder value*. Public value is what the organization does, can, or should create that the public (or parts of it) values in a collective sense. The focus is on shared or collective benefits.

sponsors   People (typically, top positional leaders) who have the prestige, power, and authority to commit the organization to implementing strategies and the strategic plan and to hold people accountable for doing so.

stakeholder   Any person, group, or organization that can place a claim on an organization's attention, resources, or output or is affected by that output.

strategic management   The integration of strategic planning and implementation across an organization (or other entity) in an ongoing way to enhance the fulfillment of mission, meeting of mandates, and sustained creation of public value.

strategic planning   A deliberative, disciplined effort to produce fundamental decisions and actions that shape and guide what an organization (or other entity) is, what it does, and why it does it. Strategic planning is an approach to dealing with the serious challenges that organizations, parts of organizations, collaborations, and communities face.

strategy   The means by which an organization intends to accomplish a goal or objective. It summarizes a pattern across policies, programs, projects, decisions, and resource allocations.

summative evaluation   An evaluation focused on making summary judgments about effectiveness.

theory of change   An explanation of what is required to bring about a desired change and how an entity expects to reach a long-term goal. A theory of change defines the underlying logic of the connections between preconditions and planned interventions.

values   Principles, beliefs, and the like that form an important part of the foundation on which an organization operates. *Value statements* answer these questions: How do we want to conduct our business? How do we want to treat our key stakeholders? What do we really care about—that is, value? Values are a part of an organization's culture, so there may very well be a difference between the values people *espouse* and the values they actually follow *in practice*.

vision statement   A description of what an organization and key parts of the external environment will look like if the organization succeeds in implementing its strategies and achieves its full potential. Often this statement includes the organization's mission, basic philosophy and core values, goals, basic strategies, performance criteria, important decision-making rules, and the ethical standards expected of all employees. Also often called a *vision of success*. An organization may have to go through more than one cycle of strategic planning before it can develop an effective vision for itself; regardless, a full-blown vision of success is more likely to be a guide for strategy implementation than strategy formulation.

Bibliography

Adams, D. (2002). *The ultimate hitchhiker's guide to the galaxy*. New York: Random House/Del Rey.

American Society for Quality. (n.d.). Project planning and implementing tools: Plan-Do-Check-Act cycle. http://asq.org/learn-about-quality/project-planning-tools/overview/pdca-cycle.html

Anderson, M., Anderson, S. R., Laeger-Hagermeister, M., Scheffert, D. R., & Steinberg, R. (1999). *Facilitation resources*. St. Paul: University of Minnesota Extension Service.

Anderson, S. R., Bryson, J. M., & Crosby, B. C. (2000). *Leadership for the common good fieldbook*. St. Paul: University of Minnesota Extension Service.

Bachrach, P., & Baratz, M. S. (1963). Decisions and non-decisions: An analytical framework. *American Political Science Review, 57,* 947–952.

Bardach, E. (1998). *Getting agencies to work together*. Washington, DC: Brookings Institution.

Behn, R. D. (1999). The new public-management paradigm and the search for democratic accountability. *International Public Management Journal, 1*(2), 131–165.

Boal, K. B., & Schultz, P. (2007). Storytelling, time, and evolution: The role of strategic leadership in complex adaptive systems. *Leadership Quarterly, 18,* 411–423.

Bohm, D. (2004). *On dialogue*. New York: Routledge. Originally published 1996.

Bolman, L. G., & Deal, T. E. (2008). *Reframing organizations: Artistry, choice, and leadership*. San Francisco: Jossey-Bass/Wiley.

Boyne, G. A., & Chen, A. A. (2006). Performance targets and public service improvement. *Journal of Public Administration Research and Theory, 17,* 455–477.

Bryson, J. M. (2004). *Strategic planning for public and nonprofit organizations: A guide to strengthening and sustaining organizational achievement* (3rd ed.). San Francisco: Jossey-Bass/Wiley.

Bryson, J. M. (2010). The future of public and nonprofit strategic planning. *Public Administration Review, 70*(Suppl.), S255–S267.

Bryson, J. M. (2011). *Strategic planning for public and nonprofit organizations* (4th ed.). San Francisco: Jossey-Bass/Wiley.

Bryson, J. M., Ackermann, F., Eden, C., & Finn, C. B. (2004). *Visible thinking*. Hoboken, NJ: Wiley.

Bryson, J. M., & Alston, F. K. (2005). *Creating and implementing your strategic plan: A workbook for public and nonprofit organizations* (2nd ed.). San Francisco: Jossey-Bass/Wiley.

Bryson, J. M., & Alston, F. K. (2011). *Creating your strategic plan: A workbook for public and nonprofit organizations* (3rd ed.). San Francisco: Jossey-Bass/Wiley.

Bryson, J. M., & Carroll, A. R. (2007). *Public participation fieldbook*. St. Paul: University of Minnesota Extension Service.

Bryson, J. M., Crosby, B. C., & Bryson, J. K. (2009). Understanding strategic planning and the formulation and implementation of strategic plans as a way of knowing: The contributions of actor-network theory. *International Public Management Journal, 12*(2), 172–207.

Bryson, J. M., Cunningham, G. L., & Lokkesmoe, K. J. (2002). What to do when stakeholders matter: The case of problem formulation for the African American Men project of Hennepin County, Minnesota. *Public Administration Review, 62*(5), 568–584.

Bryson, J. M., Patton, M. Q., & Bowman, R. A. (2011). Working with evaluation stakeholders: A rationale, step-wise approach and toolkit. *Evaluation and Program Planning, 34*(1), 1–12.

Chait, R. P., Ryan, W. P., & Taylor, B. E. (2004). *Governing as leadership*. Hoboken, NJ: Wiley.

Chrislip, D. D. (2002). *The collaborative leadership fieldbook: A guide for citizens and civic leaders*. San Francisco: Jossey-Bass/Wiley.

Crosby, B. C., & Bryson, J. M. (2005). *Leadership for the common good: Tackling public problems in a shared-power world* (2nd ed.). San Francisco: Jossey-Bass/Wiley.

Crosby, B. C., Bryson, J. M., & Anderson, S. R. (2003). *Leadership for the common good fieldbook*. St. Paul: University of Minnesota Extension Service.

Crossan, M. M., Lane, H. W., & White, R. E. (1999). An organizational learning framework: From intuition to institution. *Academy of Management Review*, *24*(3), 522–537.

Cyert, R., & March, J. (1963). *The behavioral theory of the firm*. Englewood Cliffs, NJ: Prentice Hall.

Delbecq, A. L. (2006). The spiritual challenge of power: Humility and love as offsets to leadership hubris. *Journal of Management, Spirituality and Religion*, *3*(1), 141–154.

Deming, W. E. (1982). *Out of the crisis*. Cambridge, MA: MIT, Center for Advanced Engineering Study.

Eden, C., & Ackermann, F. (1998). *Making strategy: The journey of strategic management*. Thousand Oaks, CA: Sage.

Fisher, R., & Ury, W. (1991). *Getting to yes: Negotiating agreement without giving in* (2nd ed.). New York: Penguin.

Fitzpatrick, J. L., Sanders, J. R., & Worthen, B. R. (2004). *Program evaluation: Alternative approaches and practical guidelines* (3rd ed.). Boston: Pearson Education.

Frederickson, H. G. (1997). *The spirit of public administration*. San Francisco: Jossey-Bass/Wiley.

Hackman, J. R. (2002). *Leading teams: Setting the stage for great performances*. Boston: Harvard Business Press.

Hall, J. M., & Johnson, M. E. (2009, March). When should process be art, not science. *Harvard Business Review*, pp. 58–65.

Hill, C. J., & Lynn, L. E., Jr. (2008). *Public management: A three-dimensional approach*. Washington, DC: CQ Press.

Hill, M., & Hupe, P. (2009). *Implementing public policy* (2nd ed.). Thousand Oaks, CA: Sage.

Hughes, D. J. (Ed.). (1993). *Moltke on the art of war: Selected writings*. New York: Presidio Press.

Huxham, C., & Vangen, S. (2005). *Managing to collaborate: The theory and practice of collaborative advantage*. New York: Routledge.

Innes, J., & Booher, D. (2010). *Planning with complexity*. New York: Routledge.

International Association for Public Participation. (2007). "Spectrum of public participation." http://www.iap2.org/associations/4748/files/IAP2%20Spectrum_vertical.pdf

Johnson, D. J., & Johnson, F. P. (2008). *Joining together: Group theory and group skills* (10th ed.). Boston: Allyn & Bacon.

Kaplan, R. S., & Norton, D. P. (2004). *Strategy maps: Converting intangible assets into tangible outcomes.* Boston: Harvard Business Press.

Kelman, S. (2005). *Unleashing change: A study of organizational renewal in government.* Washington, DC: Brookings Institution Press.

Kingdon, J. W. (2002). *Agendas, alternatives, and public policies* (2nd ed.). New York: Longman.

Knowlton, L. W., & Phillips, C. C. (2008). *The logic model guidebook.* Thousand Oaks, CA: Sage.

Kotter, J. P., & Cohen, D. S. (2002). *The heart of change: Real-life stories of how people change their organizations.* Cambridge, MA: Harvard Business Press.

Kouzes, J. M., & Posner, B. Z. (2002). *The leadership challenge* (3rd ed.). San Francisco: Jossey-Bass/Wiley.

Kouzes, J. M., & Posner, B. Z. (2008). *The leadership challenge* (4th ed.). San Francisco: Jossey-Bass/Wiley.

Light, P. C. (1998). *Sustaining innovation: Creating nonprofit and government organizations that innovate naturally.* San Francisco: Jossey-Bass/Wiley.

Linden, R. M. (2002). *Working across boundaries.* San Francisco: Jossey-Bass/Wiley.

Lipman-Blumen, J. (1996). *Connective leadership.* San Francisco: Jossey-Bass/Wiley.

Mattessich, P. W. (2003). *The manager's guide to program evaluation.* St. Paul, MN: Fieldstone Alliance.

McLaughlin, J. A., & Jordan, G. B. (2010). Using logic models. In J. S. Wholey, H. P. Hatry, & K. E. Newcomer (Eds.), *Handbook of practical program evaluation* (3rd ed., pp. 55–80). San Francisco: Jossey-Bass/Wiley.

Mintzberg, H. (1994). *The rise and fall of strategic planning.* New York: Free Press.

Mintzberg, H., Ahlstrand, B., & Lampel, J. (2009). *Strategy safari: A guided tour through the wilds of strategic management* (2nd ed.). London: Financial Times/ Prentice Hall.

Mintzberg, H., & Westley, F. (1992). Cycles of organizational change. *Strategic Management Journal, 13,* 39–59.

Moore, M. H. (1995). *Creating public value: Strategic management in government.* Cambridge, MA: Harvard University Press.

Moynihan, D. P. (2008). *The dynamics of performance management: Constructing information and reform.* Washington, DC: Georgetown University Press.

Neely, R. (1981). *How courts govern America.* New Haven, CT: Yale University Press.

Neustadt, R. E. (1990). *Presidential power and the modern president.* New York: Free Press.

Niven, P. R. (2008). *Balanced scorecard step-by-step for government and nonprofit agencies* (2nd ed.). Hoboken, NJ: Wiley.

Nutt, P. C. (2002). *Why decisions fail: Avoiding the blunders and traps that lead to debacles.* San Francisco: Berrett-Koehler.

Nutt, P. C., & Backoff, R. W. (1992). *Strategic management of public and third sector organizations: A handbook for leaders.* San Francisco: Jossey-Bass/Wiley.

Patton, M. Q. (2008). *Utilization-focused evaluation* (4th ed.). Thousand Oaks, CA: Sage.

Posner, R. A. (1985). *The federal courts: Crisis and reform.* Cambridge, MA: Harvard University Press.

Project Management Institute. (2008). *A guide to the project management body of knowledge* (4th ed.). Newtown Square, PA: Project Management Institute.

Riggio, R. E., Chaleff, I., & Lipman-Blumen, J. (Eds.). (2008). *The art of followership: How great followers create great leaders and organizations.* San Francisco: Jossey-Bass/Wiley.

Riker, W. H. (1986). *The art of political manipulation.* New Haven, CT: Yale University Press.

Scharmer, C. O. (2009). *Theory U: Leading from the future as it emerges.* San Francisco: Berrett-Koehler.

Schein, E. H. (2010). *Organizational culture and leadership* (4th ed.). San Francisco: Jossey-Bass/Wiley.

Schwarz, R. M. (2002). *The skilled facilitator: A comprehensive resource for consultants, facilitators, managers, trainers, and coaches* (2nd ed.). San Francisco: Jossey-Bass/Wiley.

Senge, P. (2006), *The fifth discipline: The art and practice of the learning organization.* New York: Random House/Crown.

Seligman, M.E.P. (1998). *Learned optimism.* New York: Pocket Books.

Shamir, B., Arthur, M., & House, R. (1994). The rhetoric of charismatic leadership: A theoretical extension, a case study, and implications for research. *Leadership Quarterly, 5*(1), 25–42.

Simons, R. (1995). *Levers of control: How managers use innovative control systems to drive strategic renewal.* Boston: Harvard Business Press.

Spencer, L. (1996). *Winning through participation*. Dubuque, IA: Kendall/Hunt.

Terry, R. W. (2001). *Seven zones for leadership: Acting authentically in stability and chaos*. Palo Alto, CA: Davies-Black.

Thompson, L. (2008). *The mind and heart of the negotiator* (4th ed.). Upper Saddle River, NJ: Prentice Hall.

Weick, K. (1984). Small wins: Redefining the scale of social problems. *American Psychologist*, *39*(1), 40–49.

Made in the USA
Middletown, DE
26 March 2021